T0115003

Dancing With the Dolphin

A True Mystical Tale of Healing

KATHY SCHMIDT

BALBOA.
PRESS

A DIVISION OF HAY HOUSE

Balboa Press books may be ordered through booksellers or by contacting:

Balboa Press
A Division of Hay House
1663 Liberty Drive
Bloomington, IN 47403
www.balboapress.com
1 (877) 407-4847

Because of the dynamic nature of the Internet, any web addresses or
links contained in this book may have changed since publication and
may no longer be valid. The views expressed in this work are solely those
of the author and do not necessarily reflect the views of the publisher,
and the publisher hereby disclaims any responsibility for them.

The author of this book does not dispense medical advice or prescribe the use
of any technique as a form of treatment for physical, emotional, or medical
problems without the advice of a physician, either directly or indirectly. The
intent of the author is only to offer information of a general nature to help you
in your quest for emotional and spiritual well-being. In the event you use any
of the information in this book for yourself, which is your constitutional right,
the author and the publisher assume no responsibility for your actions.

Any people depicted in stock imagery provided by Thinkstock are models,
and such images are being used for illustrative purposes only.
Certain stock imagery © Thinkstock.

Printed in the United States of America.

ISBN: 978-1-4525-8788-2 (sc)
ISBN: 978-1-4525-8790-5 (hc)
ISBN: 978-1-4525-8789-9 (e)
Library of Congress Control Number: 2013921758

Balboa Press rev. date: 12/10/2013

Preface

This is a true story. Perhaps I should say part of a story because we all partake in many dramas during the course of a lifetime. As each plot flows seamlessly into the next, it is difficult to determine where to begin my narrative. It seems to start with a question—one, in fact, about beginnings. Where it will end, I do not yet know.

This I do know. Those of us who ask questions and receive answers need to talk about it. I am grateful that others have shared their stories, for they help me dare to live my own more authentically, knowing I am not alone.

On the surface, my life seems quite ordinary. Its form may differ in details from others. But I am learning that the world outside my eyes is not where I live my greater truth. Deep within our souls is the source of our reality. And it is here, in this quiet, holy place where we are all one.

I lived through many chapters of my journey before I was able to recognize that I even had a tale to tell. I used to see myself as small and weak. Fear ruled my life. But as I learned to listen to my own inner self and others' stories, I began to release many of those fears. I ever so gradually watched my unique plot begin to unfold.

Now at last, I am learning to tell my deepest truth. I am strong and courageous. The questions I have are important. I can plumb the depths of my own great nature to find many answers.

I share here some selected details of this part of my story. I trust that its telling may encourage someone else to recognize her unique and universal truth and then to pass along the word.

Part 1
Mystical Awakenings

Chapter 1

*I*T WAS A WARM SPRING EVENING YEARS AGO. MY PLAN WAS to shop for groceries.

I'm in a parking lot. I squeeze into a spot, grab a monster cart, and pass through parting glass doors into a stadium-sized building.

Stacks of advertised specials stand sentry to miles of chock-full aisles. I bypass the papers to find the starting gate. I glance at my watch to determine the allotted time until the cash register rings. Decisions begin. I must remember family favorites, menu ingredients, and nutritional values and then determine the price from perplexing codes. A choppy pattern emerges: weigh, decide, reconsider, return item to shelf, place new choice into cart, and then dash off to next aisle.

My temperature rises. Unbutton and remove sweater; add to cart. Oh, bread and cereals. This aisle alone could use up my remaining time. With my face warm and hands clammy, I clench my jaw and toss one item and then another into the cart and turn to the next long row before me. My stomach tightens. Just a few more aisles to go, I think, and push on.

Then suddenly, the tiny swells of fear that had been lapping at the shores of my consciousness gather into a huge wave. My legs shake, yet I feel gripped in a vise. A dreadful premonition warns me: I'm in trouble. I have to get out of here—fast! Trembling, I abandon the cart in the frozen foods section and race to my car. Hot tears stream down my face as I turn the key. The short drive home seems endless.

It was my first panic attack many years ago, but I still remember it clearly. That spring evening, I had headed out to tackle the grocery shopping while my husband stayed home babysitting. Round-the-clock care of our five-month-old and coordinating the older children's activities, while juggling the rest of my household duties, had been taking its toll. I was exhausted.

More attacks like this would plague me in the months and years that followed. At times, the tiniest apprehension could launch me into waves of panic so severe that I felt as if I were about to die. Nearly anyone might experience such terror under certain circumstances, such as seeing a truck headed straight at you or having a loaded gun pointed at your head. But only a nervous system gone haywire, like mine, would evoke this type of response from a simple disappointment or indecision.

After the first few panic attacks, I grew terrified that another one would arise. As these fears snowballed, they started to rule my life. I clung more and more to the presumed safety of my home. As the size of my world diminished, I slipped into depression.

I reached out for help, and ever so gradually, it came from loved ones, doctors, and books. Medication helped diminish the intensity and frequency of the attacks. Over the course of a few years, I became more functional. Yet I continued to struggle with intermittent bouts of anxiety and depression. And hovering in the background like an ominous dark cloud loomed the threat of those waves of terror, which could burst with a thunderclap when I least expected.

I continued researching to find solutions. The subject of reincarnation started entering my consciousness. The widespread ancient belief that we are born into the physical world not merely once but many times intrigued me. Several prominent psychiatrists had used past-life regression in their therapy. Two in particular got my attention: Dr. Brian Weiss (*Many Lives, Many Masters*) and Dr. Raymond Moody Jr. (*Coming Back: A Psychiatrist Explores Past-Life Journeys*).

Weiss and Moody disagreed somewhat in their interpretations

regarding a patient's past-life experience. However, they both believed that past-life regression could be a helpful therapeutic tool to enhance the healing process. After reading their books, I wondered whether exploring reincarnation could help me.

One day, a friend who was interested in reincarnation gave me a tape from a seminar she had attended where a psychologist guided the participants in a regression process. My friend assured me that it was simple to do and that she had found it enlightening. But I still felt uncertain about what I would do regarding a former incarnation when I felt barely capable of managing my current state. So I placed the cassette in a desk drawer, where it stayed for weeks.

Now and then, as I thought about that tape, my curiosity gathered steam. Then, one cold, gray Midwest morning, I sensed an emerging eruption. I went to my study, opened the desk drawer, and retrieved the cassette. I stared at it in my hand for a while, still apprehensive about diving into the icy waters of self-discovery. An impatient part of me thought, "Just do it!" So I put the tape into the recorder, pushed the play button, and settled into my recliner.

The calm, comforting male voice on the tape gently invited me to relax. He suggested that I find myself in another place and time. In my mind's eye, I gazed down and saw bare feet. As my mental eyes moved higher, I realized I was a dark-skinned female with long, silky black hair. I was wearing a brightly colored, loose-fitting garment and standing on a sandy beach dotted with palm trees. The vivid blue sky was cloudless; the temperature was warm. A sea breeze brushed my body. The soft sand sifted over my feet. I gazed out at the ocean and saw a mist-covered mountain on a distant shore.

Suddenly, letters flashed through my mind: "n-e-s-i-a."

"Hmmm … maybe this is Polynesia," I said, guessing.

Next, a word assaulted my consciousness: "Krakatoa." Vague recollections of a volcano emerged. My stomach tightened. This island paradise no longer seemed so idyllic, and I had lost all desire to view the next reel of the movie that was playing in my mind.

I reached for the off button, sat back quietly, and reflected on what had just happened. I felt shaken. Then a thought occurred to me. I went to the bookshelf and pulled volume K of the encyclopedia. Flipping through its pages, I found "Krakatoa," a volcano that erupted in 1893 in Indonesia. The eruption of this volcano caused tidal waves that killed thirty thousand people.

Over the years, I'd had numerous nightmares in which I'd been involved in a devastating flood. I also tended to feel fearful around large bodies of water and found movies about drowning deaths terrifying. I wondered if this tropical island scenario could have been the source of some of these fears or if my mind was just weaving together images I'd seen and heard before ... in this life. Well, the encyclopedia displayed no casualty list with my name on it. Still, this whole thing was unsettling. I closed the book and put it back on the shelf.

A couple of weeks later, I awoke one morning feeling afraid and frustrated as I recalled a puzzling dream. I recorded this nighttime drama in my journal and entitled it (a tip suggested to me several years earlier at a dream seminar):

The Beast at the Beach

> I am at the beach with a large party of people. Suddenly, I feel terrified. A young man in the group displays a weapon, which he uses to threaten everyone. Somehow, I manage to get away from the crowd and begin searching for a place of refuge. I find myself in a dark, unkempt apartment badly in need of repair. And worst of all, there are clusters of strangers around, cluttering up my house. I feel annoyed and disturbed by them.

I wondered if the dream had anything to do with my fear of the tidal wave in the tropical island scenario. I had no idea who the violent young man (the beast) or all the other unwanted people in my house were.

After this beach dream, my curiosity about reincarnation intensified. I thought about my friend Suzy who had endured a puzzling near-death experience. In order to help sort it all out, she had seen a local psychologist who used past-life regression in his therapy. In my notebook, below the dream notes, I wrote, "Talk with S about shrink."

☙

I've always enjoyed writing and occasionally kept a personal journal. In its pages, I felt free to record my thoughts, feelings, inspirations, and dreams. When I was in a particularly poetic mood, I would express my ideas in verse. Around the time I began exploring reincarnation, several journals were stashed in my desk drawer. However, at this point, journaling wasn't a regular habit, just an occasional practice.

One of my journals contained an occasional experiment, which I had first tried about a year earlier after an elderly gentleman from one of my study groups showed me his notebook. In its pages, he wrote a thought or prayer to God. He then followed it with God's response to him. This lovely man was wise and spiritual-minded. His beautiful notebook pages were uplifting. Yet, I couldn't help thinking that he was a little arrogant in his belief that God was speaking to him and/or through him. Still, I felt an inner urging to attempt this same practice. So, now and then, I listened for the voice of God, and if I sensed something, I recorded it in my journal.

This process required that I concentrate on becoming quiet and peaceful. Then I began to listen intently to my spirit, the divine part of me. If a word or two came to my consciousness, I jotted it down. Sometimes more words followed. I quickly discovered my censor, the voice in me who usually said I was just making it all up or it sounded stupid. I had to let go of such thoughts. I found this practice somewhat like closing my eyes and trying to walk. I could take only one step at a time. Trust was essential. I had to believe that the universe was friendly and I was being guided. And that was difficult.

One day not too long after my inner trip to the Indonesian island, I went to my journal. In it, I wrote about feeling called to a deeper, closer walk with God and my yearning for clearer guidance and greater healing. Then in a prayerful, meditative state of mind, I tried to let go of all other cares and allowed distractions to drift away. I listened intently for a response to my request. These words came.

> *h.s. Take my hand. Do not look far down the road—only a few steps ahead. This is where I shine my light. This is where the opportunity for healing abounds—this moment, this step, and this breath. If you practice, you will learn. Welcome.*[1]

---

1 I use the initials "h.s." to indicate "higher self" or "Holy Spirit." These are the inspired writings in my journal that came during my meditative times of deep listening. I italicize them throughout the text.

Chapter 2

$\mathcal{F}$OR MANY OF US, SMALL GROUPS HAVE BECOME THE churches of today. It is a time when institutions of employment and religion have swelled to an impersonal size and family members often live far from one another. While the desire for community remains a deep personal need, finding it has become increasingly difficult. So, clusters of people from various places, backgrounds, and religions are gathering together. Some of us were led to small groups because of a common interest or experience, an illness or addiction. What most of us truly share, however, are questions in our minds and longing in our hearts for answers, connection, and healing.

The bibles for some of these new communities might be a twelve-step publication or a best-selling blend of psychology and spirituality from authors like Melody Beattie, Marianne Williamson, or N. Donald Walsch. Services could be held in conference and meeting rooms or in libraries, restaurants, hospitals, and living rooms across the country and around the world.

As a child, I was brought up in a traditional church, which met my religious needs for many years. But as I matured, my heart began resonating to a different kind of spirituality. After much soul-searching, I finally made the difficult decision to break my ties to the church of my youth. For a short time, I drifted on a lonely sea as I longed for a community of similarly minded spiritual seekers. Soon, a light pointed my way home as I was led to several small groups of people who met regularly to study spiritual ideas, share their personal journeys, meditate, or pray.

Some of my fellow travelers no longer attended church, while others were affiliated with religious institutions, both traditional and otherwise. The locations, faces, and focus of my groups changed now and then, but the warm, nurturing support they provided remained. When I sought feedback or help on many issues of my life, this was where I often brought my observations and questions.

While still a member of my childhood church, I discovered *A Course in Miracles*, a huge manuscript that two New York psychologists introduced to the world in the 1970s. Sometimes referred to as spiritual psychotherapy, the *Course* combines elements of Eastern and New Thought ideology. It speaks of relationship as a path to God and forgiveness as a requirement. Its language, much of it written in iambic pentameter, is seldom easily understood. However, for millions of people, its pages have provided many satisfying answers.

One evening shortly after my first attempt to uncover a past life, I brought my friend's regression tape to my Monday night *Course* group. At that time, there were only four or five regular members. I told them about my tropical island scenario. They expressed a curiosity about the subject, so we dimmed the lights, made ourselves comfortable, and began playing the cassette. Before long, I found myself in another place and time.

I look down at my feet and see moccasin-like boots. Layers of heavy, furry clothing cover me. My surroundings are freezing cold. I seem to be an Eskimo woman whose family includes a mother, a young male child, and a husband who is away on a hunting/fishing expedition. I watch myself go through this cold, drab existence. I envision working on a colorful rug. This small, Eskimo village is a close-knit community. I hear them singing a song about their members who are away. At the end of

*this scenario, I witness my own death at an old age from
some kind of stomach ailment.*

The tape ended. We turned on the lights and began sharing what each of us had experienced. Debbie described a peaceful meditation, but she did not discover a past life. Suzy found herself in one of the lives she had previously encountered at her therapist's office. The tape so relaxed Richard that he had drifted into an enjoyable nap

This second past life for me in its freezing setting was not as appealing as the tropical island, but at least no volcano was looming in the distance. Again, I questioned myself as to the meaning of this scenario. I told the group about my "Beast at the Beach" dream. Suzy, a psychiatric nurse by profession, repeated how much she respected her therapist, who had used the regression process in her therapy. She suggested I contact him to help me sort it all out, so I wrote down his phone number. Even though the prospect of seeing a new shrink was not appealing, I decided after a while that it was probably a good idea to get some professional help.

Dr. Lippman's office was on the second floor of a narrow two-story building in a small shopping center. After climbing the steps, I headed down a well-lit hallway and found the door to his small outer office. Inside was a row of chairs, an aquarium, some magazine racks, and a frosted window. I stood tapping my knuckles on the glass and my foot on the floor as I waited for a response.

A young, dark-haired woman slid the window back and smiled at me. I announced my name and then, looking at my watch, added, "Sorry I'm a little early." She handed me a pen and some papers and asked me to fill them out. I sat down and began writing.

"Of course I'm early. I always allow extra time to find a new doctor. Does that make me neurotic?" I asked myself, gliding easily into the self-analytical mode I sensed would be appropriate for the approaching visit. I didn't answer my own question, but just continued completing the forms and handed them back to the secretary.

I picked up a magazine, sat down, and began flipping through it. Then I distracted myself with the antics of the aquarium residents, but I had a hard time concentrating on anything. I decided to stage a brief rehearsal in my mind of the material I wanted to cover with the therapist.

Act one of my mental script contained a colorful cast of characters: one depressed, angry mother; a quiet, meek father; a firstborn Miss Perfect played by me; and two rebellious younger siblings who resented my star billing. As the play went on, I stepped into another role (critic) and labeled this drama "dysfunctional." The rest of the troupe did not appreciate my review.

I quickly scanned my stormy adolescent years and found it amazing that I had somehow survived. As I fast-forwarded to adulthood, the plot became more complicated when I began starring in a "married with children" role. This one became extremely challenging because I often felt like a child myself.

What concerned me most that afternoon as I waited in Dr. Lippman's office was the depression and panic attacks that I had experienced in varying degrees for some time. Medication helped. But there were side effects. I had gone off the meds now and then, but the anxiety/depression and bouts of panic inevitably returned before long. I felt somehow ashamed of my need for drugs. At the time, I did not recognize my destructive need to be perfect and the terrible lack of compassion I had for myself.

At the end of my mental review, I tried putting a lighter spin on these somber tales. I pictured myself on the phone to Oprah, proclaiming what luck she was in.

"All you have to do is book me," I said, "and I can provide more than enough material for a week's worth of shows."

My conversation with Oprah was interrupted as the inner office door opened. A short, nice-looking man with dark blond, thinning hair, bright blue eyes, and a warm, friendly smile walked out with his hand extended. I shook it timidly. Dr. Lippman directed me into his modest office, which housed a couch, a recliner chair, a desk displaying several family photographs, a swivel chair, and a bookcase. I smiled to myself as I noted, among the pictures on his walls, a beach scene.

After a few minutes of chitchat, the doctor asked me for some personal background, so I started with my childhood and worked up quickly to the present. I told him I was a full-time homemaker and wife/mother who had done some secretarial work. I also described several creative hobbies, such as songwriting, painting, and music, along with some occasional volunteer positions.

Next Dr. Lippman asked, "So, what brings you here today?"

"Well, I've had some severe challenges with anxiety and depression." I replied. "Medication can help, but I don't like the side effects. I've recently stopped taking the meds mainly for that reason"

"So, what have you done to replace them?" he questioned.

I thought a bit and answered, "I've been exercising more often. And I'm also trying to meditate daily."

"Good." He responded simply.

I mentioned my friend Suzy. "She likes you," I said, which brought a smile to his face, "When I told her about my health issues, she encouraged me to try past-life regression with you. I've also read some books on the subject and listened to a tape about it." Next, I told him about the Krakatoa incident and my life as an Eskimo.

The therapist acted genuinely interested in what I had to say. *But, of course, that's his job,* I reminded myself.

He seemed to be writing a lot on his yellow legal pad. I found that annoying. It made me feel self-conscious about what I was saying. I later jokingly told a friend that Dr. Lippman was probably jotting reminders to himself, like what to pick up on the way home from the office. She and I found it therapeutic to keep our sense of humor, even about such serious subjects as psychotherapy.

It also helped to relieve some of my nervousness when Dr. Lippman expressed a sense of humor as well.

"Do you mind if I refer to you as a shrink?" I asked him.

"No," he said, smiling. "In fact, I sometimes tell people I'm the 'shrink who shrunk'."

It was no doubt a lighthearted, self-deprecating reference to his stature. He talked about his background and shared a couple of his own past lives. He told me that this regression process had been emotionally helpful to quite a few of his clients. He also spoke of his Jewish heritage and said he had found more spirituality in recent times through his therapeutic experiences with clients than in previous years in synagogue.

As the session was winding down, he assured me that I'd do just fine with this regression process, which he'd planned for the next appointment. On my way home, I reflected that things hadn't gone too badly.

I later wrote in my notebook that I still felt a little afraid. Could it be a fear of discovering that I had drowned in a previous life? Or maybe it was just a generalized fear of the unknown. I recalled the encouragement given by friends who had explored their own past lives. And then, I asked for help. As I listened for a response, these words came and I recorded them.

> h.s. Dear one, do not fret. Do not be afraid. You are on
> a well-lit path. Angels surround you. They rejoice to see
> the journey begin and continue to healing. Listen and
> release. Soften, float, and stay in awareness of the person
> you are and who goes with you. Flower petals are strewn
> on the path beneath your feet. There is nothing refused
> you in your quest for wholeness. Go in peace.

Despite such reassuring messages, by the time my next appointment with the therapist arrived, I still felt tense and uneasy about this process. After a little preliminary discussion of the week's events, Dr. Lippman began doing the regression process.

"Relaxation is important," he said, "so peaceful music"—he put a tape into the recorder—"can be helpful. And I'm going to light some incense, too. Remember, your higher self knows exactly what you need and wants only good for you."

"Have you ever sought the help of a spirit guide?" he asked softly.

"No," I replied. But then I recalled a close friend who had had such an experience during her recovery from cancer and I asked the therapist if this was an example.

"Anyone can ask, but each person's prayer may result in a different outcome," he answered. "But know that help is available."

"Just lean back in the chair and try to make yourself very comfortable."

He was quiet for a bit and then began leading me through relaxation exercises and encouraged me to look back through different periods of my present life. But no matter what he said, I remained uptight.

"Try to remember your life as a teenager," he suggested.

I began to feel weepy, but I would not let myself cry. During the session, some bright colors flashed through my mind, and at one point, I saw a white dove and a flower. But it seemed insignificant. I'd had enough.

"I'm sorry," I said, "but this just isn't working for me."

We talked a little more and I expressed disappointment at what had just occurred...or rather *not occurred*.

"Each process is exactly as it's meant to be," Dr. Lippmann reassured me.

Well, that sounds rather nice, I thought, but frankly, I'd had other plans for my process.

"How about if we give it another try next time?" he suggested.

"That sounds fine," I answered weakly. But the idea of going through even one more anxiety-ridden session like this sounded unappealing. However, on the way out, I reluctantly scheduled another appointment for two weeks later and made my escape. I could just call back in a few days and cancel. This past-life thing was adding up to a big, fat zero!

Chapter 3

$\mathcal{W}$HILE I HAD BEEN DASHING ABOUT ON A QUICK TOUR of Past Life Highway, another part of me remained rambling along in the slow lane, as usual. But no matter how fast any facet of my life was proceeding, I was seldom content with staying on the surface for long. I've always known there was much more within and beyond me, and I wanted to explore.

I had read many books that stated what a valuable tool meditation was for spiritual growth, and I had tried it myself for brief periods. But I'd quickly learned it took dedication and lots of practice, and I usually ended up abandoning the process before it had become a habit. Something this time, however, gave me a confidence that I could become a true believer and make meditation a regular part of my life. On a practical level, I was looking for ways to relax, to keep away the anxiety and depression that troubled me. On a higher plane, I hoped that taking time to be still and to contemplate my vast, eternal nature could help put my issues and concerns into a universal perspective. My goal was learning to not sweat the small stuff.

At first, meditation felt awkward. The world tells us that we have to be doing something in order to be okay. I had to convince myself that it was good to just be. I often felt fidgety merely sitting in a chair. Bringing my focus back to my breath was necessary time after time. Gradually, I began adjusting to the process, and before long, it became a regular part of my routine. This period when I allowed my mind to let go of worldly concerns and consciously invited God into my heart became an important part of my day. I usually had my notebook nearby so I could record significant thoughts, feelings, or mental pictures that came up as I went into the stillness. One day, I asked if I were on the right path. This message came to me.

> *h.s. You have begun. Beginning can be very difficult, even the most difficult. You walk not alone. Remember this. Today is all there is. Simply allow it to unfold. Allow blessings to gently dance upon your head and cool, relax, and nourish your body. There is nothing to fear ever. You are safe. I love you. I am here in your breath and your thoughts. Trust me, for I am you.*

Shortly after the therapist's first regression session, I began to notice something strange occurring during my meditation periods and at other times as well. I started to sense that I was not alone. Over the course of several days, the images of three characters kept occurring in my thoughts, like a melody that slips uninvited into my mind and would not leave. It was strange and bewildering. One of my visitors was a white dove like the one I'd seen in the therapist's office. The second, a tall, regal female, arrived with these puzzling words, "Persephone, the blue goddess." Say what? The third figure needed no explanation. It was a beautiful dolphin, with whom I quickly became close friends, and whom I referred to lovingly and simply as Dolfi.

I recalled my session when the therapist had suggested that I could request help from a spirit guide. I concluded that this strange trio had come to me in response to my prayer. As these figures wove their way in and out of my consciousness, I expanded my meditation period. I would set the stage, so to speak, and then invite my guides to accompany me on inner journeys. I saw these visualizations as a kind of daytime dreaming, a process in which I allowed a part of me to create a story without my conscious direction. Like dreams, these moments also had some deep, symbolic meaning at times.

The ocean is a mysterious, even mystical place. The dolphin was often in my thoughts, so I felt drawn to inner beach trips. Dolfi quickly became my friend, advisor, and much more.

> *Dolfi is swimming playfully in my mind's ocean. He calls me to join him. After we swim a while, he says, "Let's go deeper." He jumps high and dives straight into the water. I surprise myself by diving right in after him. I'm usually uncomfortable, even fearful, in large bodies of water, but this experience feels like an adventure. As I follow my dolphin guide, he swims downward in a circular fashion, as if traveling round and round a large pole. Each time he circles, he goes deeper into the murky water, and I follow right behind him. I feel puzzled in so doing, noting that this type of experience should make me fearful. Instead, the deeper I descend, the more relaxed my whole body becomes. I gradually enter into a blissful state of peace. Dolfi then makes a mysterious statement. "Your healing is in the water."*

I began reading everything I could find about mystical experiences and spirit guides. I wondered what part my imagination was playing in these scenarios. Indeed, what exactly was imagination, this mysterious faculty that Albert Einstein called "more important than knowledge"? I kept looking for validation that what I was experiencing was real. These new phenomena in my life made me feel exhilarated and excited. But I was also confused and a little overwhelmed at times. I wanted to trust myself, but I felt hesitant. I continued recording my thoughts and feelings in my journal anyway and frequently asked for guidance. The following reassuring message hinted of things to come:

h.s. Do not be afraid. It is hard to learn to trust each moment, each word, and every breath. You shall continue. You are fine. You want only good and only peace. It is your sacred right. Know this. Be prepared at all times for inspiration to come. Be open at any moment for the burst of light to pour upon you, for the warmth of heaven to flood your soul. Hear the good word of salvation in the wind, the call of eternity coursing through your veins, and the power of the universe in the rain. Hear. Listen. Be still. Be healed.

It was not only at meditation time when my guides, especially the dolphin, came to me. If I were out somewhere and those painful, familiar feelings of anxiety threatened to overtake me, I tried calling on Dolfi. As he appeared, he would gently provide reassurance and somehow helped me to relax.

Though I sometimes tried, I could not make these guides appear or do my bidding. Instead, they just seemed to show up when I needed help. One day, the dolphin said softly that everything was all right and he loved me. It caught me off guard, and I felt touched and tearful. From the beginning, a great part of their message was simply this: "Relax, my dear. Let go. Give up trying to control everything and everyone around you."

A friend in Phoenix had told me a little about some of her mystical experiences, so I called her and poured out my tale of past lives, spirit guides, and concern for my sanity. Sara had been using visualization exercises while recovering from cancer when her guide appeared to her as a young man dressed in a toga and sandals like a youthful Jesus. She had regular conversations with her "angel" and related many of her heart's fears and longings. In the process, she discovered much about herself, including her deep desire to be a writer, a dream she has since pursued. By the end of our lengthy phone call, my bosom buddy and I laughingly concluded that we might be far out somewhere in aerie-faerie land, but the good news was that we were not alone.

Early on in one of my visualization experiences, I felt at first a little troubled.

> *The sun has just set on my inner beach scene. My surroundings are dark. I search for Dolfi, but I cannot find him. I begin to feel afraid and want to leave. Then I look to the sky above and see my dove circling there. I reach upward, and I am lifted high above the beach and taken to rest on a cloud above the darkness.*

When I wrote about this in my journal, a message came.

> *h.s. It is helpful to remember to ask for protection before you enter your meditative state. Encircle yourself with the white light. Your fear is a sign only of something deep. Do not fret. One of your guides can always help. This kind of fearful state is a familiar, difficult one for you, but you will be led step by step out of the fear. Take my hand. Always ask for help. Do not panic. Do not let the darkness pull you in. Do not focus only on the darkness. But do not race to escape either. Simply ask to be shown the way out, and it will be given you.*

Sometimes, I just asked for some words of wisdom, and I received reassuring thoughts to reflect upon. One day, I brought a problem to my meditation time, and I received this answer.

> *h.s. Know this. You are loved. Release fear. Don't focus on it. Walk through it as a foggy mist to the light. Your challenges are a golden opportunity to return to your source. Each opportunity is the rung of a golden ladder. Lift your foot from one to the next, and you will fly free to heaven.*

A musician friend and I had been writing and recording songs together for a couple of years. Though we had not succeeded in getting our work published, she had performed some of our creations at her church where she was the musical director. Our collaboration had been a delightful, creatively fulfilling process for me and her as well. Around this time, however, my associate had become very busy with some other endeavors and did not seem to have time for our regular sessions together. Life is about continual change. I knew that in my head. I just wished that some changes were easier to accept with my heart. Reluctantly, I had to admit that our partnership had probably played itself out.

One day after talking with my songwriting friend, I found myself wishing that I could just let go of this experience and go on with the flow of life's inevitable transitions. But old abandonment issues crept into my consciousness. I went to my quiet time, feeling a little hurt and sad.

> Today at the beach, I am in a sad mood. Soon, my dolphin guide appears, playing joyfully in the water. He asks me to join him. After some hesitation, I reluctantly follow him for a swim. In a little while, Dolfi abruptly turns around and moves toward me. Then he stands up, bows, and asks politely, "Shall we dance?" This move catches me completely by surprise. What can I say or do? It all seems so silly that I start to laugh. Then something within nudges me to change course. So I stand tall, bow my head, and reply warmly, "Well, sure, Dolfi. I'd be delighted." Strains of music float on water-sprayed air. I reach out for my friend, and he leads me gliding through the waves. The tension I had been feeling starts to fade. My spirit lightens, and my outlook brightens as my dear dolphin guide lifts and leads me swirling through a wet, yet unforgettable, waltz.

As time went by, I grew more grateful for the presence of these unusual companions in my life. I was unaware that I would soon need all the help I could get because of a revelation that was about to occur.

Chapter 4

$\mathcal{M}$Y DREAMS OFTEN CONTAINED FOGGY IMAGES OF people from my past. But this one was especially vivid.

An Obstacle in My Path

While at a party, I am surprised to see Greg, a boyfriend from many years ago. I wave and begin walking toward him. A large, mean-looking woman steps forward and puts her hand out to stop me. "He didn't recognize you!" she growls. I ask, "What do you mean? Of course he did. Look! He's smiling at me!" What's wrong with this crazy woman? I continue trying to move forward, but I am unable to reach this old flame of mine. The stern woman's words seem so odd. I have no idea what they mean.

Shortly after the dream, this vision arose during my meditation.

I am at a lovely, deserted stretch of beach. My dolphin comes out of the water and lies beside me. I begin reviewing various stages of my life. So many times I felt like I was on the outside of events, just looking in. I seldom seem to belong. As I focus on negative aspects of my life, lonely feelings arise. Dolfi tries to comfort me.

I asked what I could learn from this scene, and I received this response.

> h.s. Each part of your life is a perfect development. As you look at it with love, you will see that. Pain makes no sense, but love does. Your life, as all lives, is a search for love. And yet, love is your essence and the reason why you are here. But mists shroud our vision until we are enlightened. Love is all. You have always been loved, are loved, and will be loved forever. Know that. Learning that is why you are here.

Soon after, in a meditative scene, several young men appeared with whom I'd had romantic relationships long ago. I wondered why all this old stuff was being dredged up. Sure, my sexuality was a highly charged, often challenging part of my life. But I assumed most people had such issues. It didn't seem like a big deal. Or was it?

My recent dream and the visualization blended, and something began bubbling to the surface in the pond of old memories.

I was fifteen; Greg was seventeen. We were too young for a serious relationship, but we fell in love anyway, though most might call it "puppy love." It was a time—the late fifties—when girls were often labeled good or bad depending on their so-called reputation. I was determined to remain one of the good girls in spite of my recently discovered sexual feelings. And yet I soon learned that Greg was a very possessive young man. After we had dated a year or so, I could no longer handle his intensity, so we broke up. During the next couple of years, I dated others but still managed to retain my so-called good girl designation. This was probably due, at least in part, to the nuns' dire warnings of sin and eternal damnation and my mother's morbid tales of pregnancy and childbirth.

The summer after I graduated from high school, I found Greg edging his way back into my life. The fires of our mutual attraction were reignited. I assumed that, because I was older, I would be able to handle this tempestuous relationship. I was wrong. One muggy July evening, Greg invited me out and we went to a large outdoor party. I was not feeling well, just getting over a sinus infection and still taking prescribed medication. At the party, there were plenty of alcoholic beverages, and I recall having at least one. Not long after, the evening's memories remain blurry. My next clear awareness was in the early hours of the morning when Greg's voice was rousing me from a semiconscious state. I was a mess, mentally and physically. We were in his car in front of my house. I somehow managed to find my way to my room and into bed that night.

The next morning, the sun nudged me reluctantly from sleep. As splinters of memory began piercing my mind and heart, I wanted so badly to believe it was just a horrible dream I'd been having. Instead, ever so gradually, I awakened to the awful truth. It was not a dream.

That previous night, I had somehow fallen into a vulnerable state, and someone I cared for and trusted had taken intimate advantage of me. I felt ashamed. How could I have allowed this to happen? Crying, I called Greg and begged him to tell me. Why? He said little about the night before except to assure me that, if I were pregnant, he would marry me. How could I think of marrying someone who had treated me so unlovingly?

The term "date rape" was unheard of when I was a teenager. It was assumed then that the perpetrator of a rape was nearly always someone the victim did not know. Even though I had not consented to the sexual incident that night, I was close to Greg and had agreed to our date. So, the idea that he had raped me was a foreign idea at first. In order to find some meaning in this nightmare, I began to craft a new version of the truth. In the process, I almost managed to convince myself.

"It was my fault. I shouldn't have taken the drink(s)."

All my life, I had felt such a deep sense of responsibility for everyone and everything. So when looking for someone to blame, I naturally pointed the finger at myself. How little I thought of myself! I had not even considered the possibility that this young man had a responsibility to do the right thing.

"It wasn't so bad."

The alcohol/medication mix must have caused me to black out for a while. Maybe that was good. Wasn't it? Well, it had kept me from consciously experiencing any physical pain at the time. But I was overlooking the deeper part of me, which knows and carries all that happens to me.

"At least it wasn't a stranger."

Yes, my violator was someone I knew, maybe even loved. So, what would that teach me about relationships, intimacy, and trust, lessons I would spend a lifetime unlearning?

I somehow got through the next hours, days, and weeks with the terrible fear of pregnancy clouding every waking moment. It was a time before home tests. I was planning to begin college in a couple of months on a scholarship. It was the only way I could ever have had such an opportunity. And now suddenly, because of this one terrible night, my entire future was in jeopardy.

When I at last realized with relief that I was not pregnant, I did the only thing I was capable of at that time. I took this awful incident and buried it somewhere very deep inside of me. My repression was so effective that, for more than thirty years, only a tiny part of me barely remembered that this trauma had ever happened. I never talked about it, even to my closest friends. Many times, I heard women speak of their rape experience and saw many such ordeals depicted on film, yet never once did I identify with the victim.

Rape happened to someone else, I thought. *Not to me!*

After this issue had been brought to light, I thought back to a time about ten years after the rape. I had two young children, and my marriage was troubled. During this difficult period, I had an intensely vivid dream.

It is winter, and snow covers the ground. A funeral procession makes its way from outside into a church. As the casket is carried, I see bright red blood dripping out

onto the whiteness below. I feel a chill as I realize who is
in the casket. It is Greg, my ex-boyfriend.

At the time, I had no idea what this dream meant. I recounted it to a friend, who said something about death meaning new beginnings. Her words did little to enlighten me. Now, these many years later, I recognized that my deeper self had been pointing to the source of some of my problems. The dream was revealing that, despite my attempts to bury this issue, it was still alive and causing me emotional pain. At last, I was able and willing to shine a light on the truth of that muggy July evening so long ago.

Too much action had been filling my soul's drama—past lives, vivid dreams, mystical meditations, spirit guides, and repressed memories. It felt like I was on some kind of cosmic roller coaster. A part of me was yelling, "Cut!" But when I was very still, I could hear another quiet voice asking me to listen.

At the beach, I see a gigantic whale far away in the ocean.
Dolfi swims from the whale toward me. He leaps high
into the air and tosses a fish to the dove flying nearby.
The next thing I know, I am transported high into the
heavens. I look down and watch the tiny earth spinning
around. I think, "Can I find myself on the planet?" A
word comes to me. "Cana." "That's strange," I think.
I know this is the site recorded in the New Testament
where Jesus of Nazareth performed his first public
miracle. I am soon transported to a time long ago. I
walk along a dusty street by a series of small buildings.
I hear music and follow it inside. People dressed in
colorful robes laugh and dance to mark a celebration. I
look around. And then I see him in the midst of a small

group of people who are focusing intently on his every
word. A shadow falls across the man's face. He sees me
staring at him, turns his head, and smiles. He starts to
walk toward me. My heart swells. As he comes closer, his
presence—strong yet gentle—overwhelms me. Finally,
as he stands directly before me, I recognize this magnetic
being as Jesus. Compassion and love fill his eyes. He lifts
his hand and tenderly touches my cheek. I start to cry.

I lingered in my meditation chair, still feeling the safety and warmth of a loving embrace. I thought back to the decision I'd made some seven years earlier to leave my childhood church. It had been difficult to pull away from my tribal roots, despite my belief that it was the right thing for me to do. I recalled the pain I felt when others criticized me for making that choice. I realized that I, too, was wrong when, at times, I judged others for their religious beliefs.

When I used to hear people talk about a relationship with Jesus, I wondered what that meant exactly. Sometimes, it even seemed that, when I turned my back on the Church, I threw out the baby (Jesus) with the bath water. But all I had really done was reject the image of Jesus, which I had connected with church doctrine, dogma, judgment, and politics. All had no connection with the person I encountered that afternoon as I yielded to my inner guide's leading. This Jesus was strong, kind, completely loving, and accepting of every part of me, even the parts I found unacceptable in myself.

Then something occurred to me. It was Holy Week! For most of my life, I had attended church services during this time of year. It was a time that recalled the death and resurrection of Jesus. I had not been to church in more than six years. And yet that April afternoon, I did not have to leave my room to encounter Jesus. Instead, this teacher and friend came to tell me something I desperately needed to hear. No matter where I was or what I did, I was loved! It was a message I would hear many, many times before I could take it more deeply into my heart.

My next appointment with Dr. Lippman was drawing near. I had thought of canceling it, but I changed my mind. Right after my last session, an intriguing series of inner events had begun, and I wondered if the counselor had been a sort of catalyst. Then after the repressed rape emerged, I felt even more strongly that I needed some professional help. However, I was starting to recognize one slight problem with this new therapist.

Whenever I thought of him, some disturbing feelings arose. After struggling with it a while, I had to admit that I had developed a nearly instant infatuation with my therapist. I presumed that this process was a fairly common occurrence. But I thought it would have taken a while to develop, and I'd only seen him for three hours.

Then a word came to mind that I'd read about, "transference." I wondered if that was what was happening. I recalled a friend of mine who underwent therapy a few years earlier. I used to be puzzled at her nearly constant anger at and complaints about her therapist. She had told me that her father had abused her as a child, and she seemed to be transferring that rage at her father on to her counselor.

I wondered if my issues surrounding the repressed rape were a part of this transference. I knew that, if I would continue seeing this therapist, I'd have to tell him about my feelings. But what would I say? "I have a crush on you." That felt so "schoolgirlish" and embarrassing. My life just kept getting more and more complicated.

At my next counseling appointment, I asked a question. "Tom [he had suggested I call him by his first name], do you pray for your clients?"

"Why? Would you like me to pray with you now?" he asked.

"No." I said, startled. "I was just looking for an explanation for all that's been happening. I know you're an openly spiritual person and that prayer can be powerful."

I told him about the three spirit guides and described my visualization experiences. Then I described meeting Jesus and how moving it had been. He was listening very attentively.

Then he said quietly, "You know, you're being reborn."

I did not know how to respond.

"Well, this may surprise you," he said, "but Jesus has appeared to some of my clients. Right here in this office."

Surprised? Stunned was how I felt about this statement from my Jewish therapist!

I described the dream about my old boyfriend and revealed the fateful summer evening when I was assaulted. As Dr. Tom listened, he looked disturbed.

After I finished, I added quickly, "I've forgiven Greg."

Then my counselor asked gently, "Have you forgiven yourself?"

At that moment, I didn't know what to say. But I knew this was an important question. "There's something else I need to talk about. I don't know exactly how to say this. Or even if I should."

His eyes widened.

I started talking about how I'd often felt kind of uneasy, even threatened, when I was around men. And I wondered if it were some kind of an issue with me. Next, I think I mentioned something about getting in touch with my male energy. I thought this must have sounded stupid, and I was not even sure what I was saying. I stumbled over my words a bit longer and then finally managed to spill out how I was attracted to him and how uncomfortable it made me feel. I was expecting him to laugh, but he looked serious.

Then I asked, "Is this some kind of transference?"

He raised his eyebrows, shrugged a little, and tilted his head. He seemed to be saying, "Maybe so."

"I'm glad you told me," he said softly. "I want you to know that you're perfectly safe with me."

Safety wasn't on my mind. But then, I had heard of unethical doctors who took advantage of vulnerable clients. So, it was good that he reminded me of that. I was just grateful at that moment to have gotten this disturbing issue out in the open where we could deal with it. My relief was short-lived, however. I tensed up as I realized it was time for another attempt at regression. I began wondering what else was going to come out in the open.

Chapter 5

I MOVED TO THE RECLINER IN THE THERAPIST'S OFFICE and tried to make myself comfortable. Letting go of control, which this process required, was extremely difficult for me. After what seemed like a very long time, I was finally able to relax a little. Then, in a while, I found myself transported someplace far away.

> *It looks like the same tropical island I had visited in my first regression. But this time, the sky is very dark, and a fierce wind is blowing about the palm trees. As I watch the ocean waters churning, a tidal wave comes to mind. I start to tremble.*

"I'm afraid," I said.
"Don't fight it," Dr. Tom said to me. "Just go with it."
Instead, I tensed up. I felt frightened. I wanted to run away.

> *Suddenly, I think of Dolfi and call for him. As soon as he appears to me, the storm abates, the ocean calms, and the sun begins to shine. I feel relieved. "Good. I can relax now," I think. But it doesn't last long. Once again, I find myself in the scenario where I am an Eskimo. I start shivering, and my teeth are chattering.*

The therapist gave me a blanket, but it didn't help. I was freezing cold and wanted to get out of there, too. I changed my mental focus and started to rest a little. Dr. Tom encouraged me to continue.

Soon, I find myself high in the heavens. I have a momentary flash of being on a magic carpet, but it seems silly, so I ignore it.

"I want to find myself on the earth, but I'm afraid," I said.
"What are you afraid of?" Dr. Tom asked.
"I don't know," I answered. "I just don't trust myself."

Gradually, the carpet floats back into my consciousness. I get on it and allow it to take me to my next location. Next, I find myself in a hot, busy marketplace swarming with people in long robes. "It feels Asian," I think.

"Maybe Middle Eastern," I said, thinking aloud. "Turkey!" I exclaimed, more certain.

The scene is vivid. There are flutes, bells, animal noises, and people haggling about prices. The smells—tobacco, fragrant perfumes, and spices—are rich.

"It's so exotic," I declared excitedly, caught up in the colorful atmosphere. And then, impulsively, I added, "Even erotic." At once, I felt embarrassed.
What has gotten into me? I thought.
"Are you male or female?" Dr. Tom asked.
"Female," I replied.
"How old?" he asked.
"Young. My skin is dark."
I saw myself covered with unsightly bumps. It felt embarrassing,

so I didn't mention it. But then, I surprised myself by saying, "I have a veil on, and I want to take it off."

Why am I saying these outrageous things? I thought.

> *The scene shifts. I am in a large room ornately hung with rich tapestries. Other women—mostly young and beautiful—are there. I feel squeamish and uncomfortable.*

"I'm in a harem," I said. "This is not a happy place. I want to get out of here."

Dr. Tom said, "Contact your spirit guide."

Just thinking of the dolphin relaxes me.

> *"Dolfi, where are you?" I call. I feel certain he will help me. As soon as I see him, I plead, "Dolfi, what should I do?" Quiet. Then, this one-word answer sends shock waves through my soul. "Dance!"*

"What kind of crazy answer is that?" I sat up abruptly, bringing my full awareness back to my therapist's office.

"Well," Dr. Tom declared, ignoring my question, "that was quite a journey!" He paused for a moment reflectively and then added softly but matter-of-factly, "You know, your sex chakra is blocked."[2]

Oh, great! I thought. *As if I don't have enough problems!*

I mumbled something about being confused and overwhelmed. The shrink suggested I try to go further with this scenario in my private meditations at home. I nodded but mentally filed that idea under "No way!" I made another appointment at the front desk and headed hurriedly out the door. My life felt shaken up and spread out

---

2   Chakras are energy centers in the body (usually seven) beginning at the base of the spine and ascending to the top of the head. They are described in Eastern philosophy and medicine.

like a giant jigsaw puzzle. How would I ever put it all together? I did not even have all the pieces.

A few days after the regression, at my quiet time, a surprising, intriguing question occurred to me. I posed it to my female spirit guide.

"What does it mean to be a woman?" I asked.

The following came to me.

> *I see myself as a young woman, a teenager. Then a series of young men whom I had dated appear to me. These images, cloudy at first, take on a sudden clarity. I feel pain and confusion as I struggle with not giving in to the persuasive nature of my sexual passion. I panic at the prospect of what could happen if I do not keep things under control: danger, rape, and pregnancy.*

Then a reassuring message...

> *h.s. Can you see how very beautiful we all are? We try to make it so complicated, but the simple reality is this: We are all just yearning for love, to give and receive love.*

My heart was touched and filled with forgiveness for myself and others. I started to cry.

The meditation continues.

> *I feel an intense, warm energy sweeping over and through me, powerful and unsettling. I don't know what is happening.*

Then, I receive a message.

> *h.s. Trust yourself. Honor your feelings. They are valid and powerful. They are true. Don't be ashamed. They are life longing for itself.*

The energy continues moving and pulsating. My body is warm—enticing yet frightening. I tried to resist the feelings. Again, words come to me.

> *h.s. Let the river of life flow through you, course through your veins, pump your heart, and move the mountains in your life. No fear. Only love. It's all there is. Rejoice. Celebrate.*

The passionate feelings continued. I wanted to stop the energy, but each time I tried to shut down, a gentle urging spoke.

> *h.s. Trust yourself. Don't run away. Be who you are, even if it's scary.*

At last, I stopped resisting and yielded to the stirrings within. I wanted to know everything about my beloved. I felt an intense yearning to give and to receive love. My desire was passionate. I wanted to hold, embrace, and unite with my beloved.

The warmth kept flowing through my body. I felt myself merging, becoming one with the beloved. The feelings were powerful and breathtaking. My passion cannot be contained. I felt the love overflowing and going forth to fill the world. The feelings were at once physical and spiritual. All was one as I was one with my beloved with the universe. Ecstasy! And then I sensed these words.

> *The cosmic dance.*

For a while, I could do nothing but sit still in silence. As I reflected on my small part in this divine mystery of life, awe filled me.

A few days later during my meditation, another intriguing question impressed itself upon me. I surprised myself once again by asking my spirit guides. "What does it mean to be a man?"

A powerful journey ensues. I start by taking a bumpy, wet ride across some huge ocean waves. Next, I am propelled into the heavens and tossed about like a feather by forceful winds. A celestial storm erupts. Lightning flashes. Thunder roars. My senses reel. Suddenly, all is quiet. I take a deep breath. In the next scene, I see my parents as they are about to create me. Then I am there as a union of egg and sperm in my mother's womb. Time speeds up. As I grow closer to birth, I begin feeling a resistance. Then I think of family members who are happily anticipating my arrival. It gives me courage to make this important journey.

I wrote in my journal, "I am going to such amazing places, and they are all within me."

Later at my meditation time, I asked my higher self, "Why is all this happening to me?"

And then I received this startling answer. *"I had to get your attention."*

During this time of the dolphin, I rarely experienced certainty about anything! Instead, it felt more often like I was walking through a field of land mines. But I knew one thing for sure. Someone had definitely gotten my attention!

Chapter 6

As I STRUGGLED TO UNDERSTAND MY EXPERIENCES, I asked for and received help in often surprising ways. As if by magic, books appeared to address various aspects of my inner drama. I had purchased some of them months, even years, earlier, and there they were, waiting there for me on my bookshelf.

In one of these enlightening books, *Seat of the Soul,* author Gary Zukav speaks of our evolution from five-sensory humans to multisensory beings. He says that authentic power is found through our hearts. Zukav suggests it is never appropriate to suppress an emotion or to disregard what one feels. By knowing what we feel, we can challenge those aspects and energies that do not serve our development.

In *Awakening in Time,* transpersonal psychologist Jacquelyn Small writes of the spiritual journey from codependence to cocreation.[3] Small discusses chakras, the Ancient Eastern system of explaining energy centers within the body. This book also describes the intense, sometimes troubling *kundalini* experience, which helped shed some light on certain aspects of my turbulent inner journey.

I wondered why my spirit guides came to me in these specific forms. The dove was pretty easy to figure out. This symbol of the Holy Spirit inspires and brings peace. In the midst of my frequent anxiety

---

3   Transpersonal psychology incorporates both Western and Eastern thought and spiritual traditions from throughout the world.

and stormy emotions, I longed for peace and inspiration. A dove can soar high above earthly problems. Such a symbol of freedom was calling me, it seemed, to release my earthbound fears and entrapments.

Dolphins are intelligent, playful, loving, even mystical creatures who call us to let go and explore the deep ocean of feelings. Though dolphins are mammals, fish surround them. My astrological sign happens to be Pisces, the fish.

"Persephone the Blue Goddess," my third spirit guide, was less prominent and more puzzling and required some research. As a goddess, she was presumably reminding me of my divinity. In Greek mythology, she was abducted by Hades and forced to live in the underworld for six months each year.

My romantic-like feelings toward the therapist still troubled me. I felt a little guilty about continuing the therapy under such conditions, yet I believed that professional help at this confusing period was important. If I were to go to a different therapist, I suspected I might just transfer the transference to him. I thought of looking for a female counselor. But that seemed like giving in to my usual pattern of evading or escaping my painful issues. My higher self had been telling me not to run away even if I felt afraid.

I had read that transference was a good thing and it even helped the process of psychotherapy. But it didn't feel right. When I thought of my therapist, I often felt a painful sadness that seemed to come from somewhere deep within, a place I had only recently accessed as I started to deal with the repressed rape. A curious part of my disturbing connection with Dr. Tom was that I could not picture his face in my mind when I thought of him.

I was planning to leave town to help my daughter move. A regression session with Dr. Tom was scheduled for after I returned. But once again, I was thinking about canceling it. I was losing interest in past lives and getting tired of the turbulent feelings the therapy was provoking in me. Shortly before I left for my trip, a passage in a book I was reading stood out. It said, "The only way out is through." I decided to keep the appointment.

Around this time, I questioned in my journal if I knew Dr. Tom in a past life.

The practice of meditation has many benefits. It's free. And it can be done anywhere and anytime. While I was in Chicago at my daughter's new apartment, I awoke early one morning. As my daughter remained upstairs sleeping, I slipped down to the living room, put on a meditative tape, and settled into an aluminum lawn chair, the only available seat. I invited Dolfi to take me where I needed to go. Soon, I found myself in a place and time far away.

I am in the Middle Eastern past life I encountered in therapy. Once again, while in the harem, I see large, ugly bumps covering my body. I realize that this symbolizes the negative way in which I see myself. I remember these words in the regression session, "I am wearing a veil, and I want to take it off." This must have been an attempt to express my poor self-esteem and the masks I was wearing. At this harem, a sultan is in charge. He has several sons, all of whom have access to the women there. I feel unhappy and trapped in this place. No one here knows the real me, it seems. I am appreciated only for what pleasure I can provide to others. However, one of the sultan's sons is different. He is kind, wise, and even holy. He speaks of spiritual truths and listens to me. He helps me believe that I am good and valuable. I am grateful, and I become enamored with this man. But I do not know how to handle my passionate feelings and become obsessed with him. Then I recognize my teacher in the past life is my therapist in this one, Dr. Tom! The rest of the scenario is unclear. I sense that something

*awful happens to the sultan's son. I feel sad and troubled
and blame myself for somehow having caused it.*

This vision had been so vivid. I felt shocked, confused, and sad about the loss of someone I loved. But there was little time for reflection that morning.

A couple of days after the harem scene, while still at my daughter's, I had this lovely meditative experience.

Dolfi takes me to a beautiful, small lake with a cascading waterfall. There, he performs a kind of ritual. He touches me reverently on each shoulder and then on my head. "Go and teach and heal," he says. I feel unworthy and reply hesitantly, "But I'm not ready." As often happens, Dolfi's response surprises me. "In doing," he says, "you will become ready."

These words stayed with me. I asked myself how I was supposed to do this teaching and healing. Through writing about my mystical experiences? Around this time, I had been thinking about finding a volunteer position. I wondered if that were the mission Dolfi referred to. Or was he simply pointing me to the small, mundane, everyday experiences that occur with my family, friends, and others? I recalled *A Course in Miracles* stating that we are all teachers to one another and we each teach what we need to learn.

Shortly after I arrived home from Chicago, our younger son, Drew, had an automobile accident. His car was totaled. Thankfully, no one was hurt. But this incident reminded me that I could not spend all my time in mystical realms. Though my spirit was homesick for heaven, my feet were tied firmly to the earth.

One day, it struck me why I had not been able to see Dr. Tom's face when I thought of him before. I did not want to "face" him, to confront and deal with those disturbing feelings of infatuation. After I uncovered the rest of the harem story, his face came more easily to my mind. The troubling transference feelings seemed to be subsiding as well. I was hoping I could wrap up this past-life search and move on.

Wouldn't it be nice if all of life's episodes were resolved in a tidy package with a big, shiny bow on top? Unfortunately, the real world does not usually provide us with happy endings like books and movies often do. Actually, I was finding the meaning of reality growing cloudier each day. If this past life in a harem were true, it could explain my nearly instant attraction to Dr. Tom. Or maybe it was just a story my subconscious made up to highlight some experiences I was having at the time. But why? I sensed there were many valuable lessons for me here. But I wanted quick answers. Perhaps I simply needed more time. My journal contained a loving reminder.

> *h.s. You cannot go backward or stand still. The direction is forward. The moment is now. Let go. Let go. Let go. Step by step and moment by moment, trust. Allow. All will unfold in perfect order. You are doing fine. You are loved. You are in your perfect place. Trust yourself, for you are me.*

I returned to my regular routine, which was comforting with its beguiling promise of predictability. My quiet, reflective moments had become an essential part of my schedule. One morning, as I listened to a tape entitled, "Sacred Space," a lovely mystical experience spoke to me of ways to walk in peace.

> *It is dusk at the beach. The sun has just slipped over the horizon. An overwhelming gratitude wells up in me for these unique companions who have led me through some healing moments. I am moved to tears. I begin thanking them over and over. I prepare a large, soft blanket for Dolfi to lie on. The dove circles lazily overhead. Persephone prepares a fire, sits by it, and stirs the logs. I feel a oneness with them and the universe. It*

is so peaceful. I ask my guides what I can do for them because they'd been doing so much for me. Dolfi says, "Stay close." The dove replies, "Be happy." Persephone tells me, "Remind yourself often of who you are. Strong and divine." I say, "Thank you. Thank you."

And then, I sensed these words, which I wrote in my journal.

h.s. Always remain grateful—to yourself, to us, to others, to God, to the universe, and to the divinity within and around you. You are learning the secrets of divine contentment. All is well.

Chapter 7

At my next counseling session, I cut short our usual preliminary chitchat.

"Guess what?" I exclaimed. "I got the rest of the harem scenario."

Dr. Tom picked up his yellow writing pad as I began describing the details of my vision, all except the ending.

Then I asked, "Do you know who the sultan's son was?"

He squinted and looked as if he were about to respond.

I plunged ahead. "It was you!"

He smiled. His eyes widened.

"This past-life stuff is intriguing, isn't it? I don't know if I actually lived any of these other lives. But they seem to be giving me some clues about this crazy journey of mine. I feel like there's a kind of war going on inside me. On one side of this battle are some very strong feelings I've been trying to suppress. They're symbolized by the tropical island, the exotic marketplace, and the harem. Then there's another opposing side of me. It's my very responsible, good girl identity. She was there in the frozen North and is terrified of being swept away by a tidal wave or having to dance in a harem. Then my inner voice is telling me to feel my feelings, not to be afraid and not to run away. I think I now understand at least part of those awful panic attacks. It was like a pressure cooker. All my repressed feelings had to come out some way, and so they exploded."

Something else came to mind. I told Dr. Tom about my previous inability to see his face clearly in my mind. "That's changed," I said, "since I got the rest of the harem scenario. Plus ..." I paused for emphasis. "Those troublesome transference feelings seem to be subsiding, too. And that's a relief."

I could think of nothing else to say. Dr. Tom was quiet, too. I finally said, "I still think there are some missing puzzle pieces." Then, after another pause, I asked, "So, where do we go from here?"

He said, "I suggest we try another regression and see what might come up."

Of course, that was his "thing." In spite of the light the regression process had shed on some issues, I still felt cautious. I started to tense up. But I couldn't think of any better idea. So I moved to the recliner.

I go to my usual seaside location. Dolfi arrives. He is unusually playful. I watch him a while. Then he tells me to become a child. I picture myself about three years old. I am wearing a one-piece orange swimsuit, playing in the sand with a bucket and shovel. Dolfi says, "Make peace with your past." I know he means the past in my present life. Then I watch various scenes from my childhood as they move by swiftly.

Dr. Tom asked, "How do you feel?"

"Lonely." I began to cry.

"What is causing your tears?"

"I don't know," I said. "I don't want to explore this." I tried to shift emotional gears. "Maybe I can go to another life," I said somewhat jokingly.

"We can do that," he answered seriously.

But soon, I realized that wasn't what I really wanted either.

"I'm just feeling confused and frustrated about that." I told him. "I'm playing the second-guessing game with myself again, wanting someone else to tell me what to do, but also wanting to be control."

"You really have a hard time making decisions, don't you? he countered.

"Yes, I'm definitely feeling "stuck. I seem to be losing interest in exploring past lives and unsure what I should do instead."

"Don't worry," he said reassuringly. "You'll be led where you need to go."

On the drive home, my mind wandered. What would it be like to live Tom's life? It seemed so perfect. Oh, sure, I knew everyone had some problems. Still, I could not imagine anything wrong in his world. I envied him and his beautiful wife. Her picture with their three daughters was always there on his desk.

Several dark, rainy days went by. I felt achy and on the verge of tears. When I went to meditate, the feelings of loss came up. I thought about my dear teacher in the harem life. Then I saw Dr. Tom in my mind. I didn't like sad feelings. But I knew that repression was not a healthy response either. I asked my higher self what was going on.

> *h.s. You may need a little more time to process and complete what you've been absorbing. Be patient. You need not know what's next at this time. Stay where you are. Love the person you are. Clear a path in front of you. Get rid of extraneous confusions and unnecessary distractions. Still your body more. Clear your mind more. A clear pond reflects the heavens. Don't throw stones in it. Let the water settle, and be still. Rest. Amen.*

My husband I have had the typical challenges of most long-term relationship couples. But we often felt like we were carrying even more than the usual baggage. We identified greatly with the books by John Gray, especially *Men Are from Mars, Women Are from Venus*. It was a relief to learn why we often felt as if each of us were from a different planet.

Over the years, some counseling and marriage enrichment experiences helped us become closer for a while. But then we'd get busy with family, work, and other commitments, and our relationship would slide down on our priority list. Before long, we would find ourselves slipping back into complacency, withdrawal, and sadness about our lack of intimacy with one another. It was not a good place to be. But it was familiar. Unfortunately, things would have to get even worse before we were willing to do what it took to make things better.

Our second-born child, first son Jonathan, seemed to be at least one of the reasons I spent many hours in prayer. Tall, handsome, funny, and smart, Jon had gone through much of his life dangling dangerously on the edge. His escapades drove me and my husband, especially me, crazy. His frequent use of alcohol concerned us. Even more troubling was our suspicion that he had at least dabbled in drugs.

Jon had graduated from college in another state a year earlier. We reluctantly invited him to move back in with us for a while, hoping we could help launch him into a straighter, more adult life. It was a well-intentioned idea, but we were starting to suspect that our plan might have just forestalled the inevitable. Eventually, he would have to grow up, take responsibility, and make healthy, adult decisions for and by himself.

When I first told my therapist about Jonny, I referred to our occasional stormy arguments.

"Are you afraid of him?" Dr. Tom asked me.

His question startled me. After some thought, I answered, "I have to admit that I am at times. Jonny and I often clash and push each other's buttons.

"You need to get him out of your home," he said, seriously. I assumed he was right. But I also realized how difficult that would be.

One day, Dr. Tom made a disturbing statement. "Some of these young people don't make it."

My heart sank. "What do you mean?" I didn't really want to hear his answer.

"They can end up strung out on drugs or even kill themselves," he responded solemnly and softly.

The doctor's words prompted my anger. Why was he was being

so negative? Was he trying to frighten or prepare me? As I heard him presenting the negative possibilities of Jon's future unless he changed his behavior, it was nearly more than I could bear. My personality self was lost in fearful imaginings. In order to find some peace, I sought the wisdom of my higher self.

> *h.s. Do not be afraid. Heavenly beings protect you. Call light to you. Surround yourself with it. Lift yourself to the finer, higher vibrations of light and love. Do not be drawn downward to heaviness. Know this. You can do whatever you are called to do. You will be given the strength, courage, wisdom, patience, love, determination, and fortitude to carry out any task that lifts you to your higher path. There is nothing to be afraid of. Breathe deeply. Relax. Appreciate. Laugh. Cry. Dance. As you are healed, you will and do extend that love and healing to those in your life and to those who will come into your life.*

One of the books I'd been reading suggested that we could get too attached to our spirit guides. I asked if anyone else were around out (or in) there. Dolfi arrived. And someone, a smaller dolphin, was with him. I referred to him as "Little Dolfi." He only stayed for a short time though. I supposed it had something to do with my needing to explore my childhood. Then one day, I met someone else.

> *It is a young child who looks like a greeting card angel. Her name, she says, is Annabelle. She invites me to go high with her in the heavens, sprinkling gold dust along the way. Then I feel a longing to go to the earth. When I do, I realize at once that I am in a different body. I see myself as my Aunt Beverly who died about five years before I, Kathy, was born. Beverly was my mother's baby sister, born when my grandmother was in her late forties.*

She was a beautiful, little, blonde, blue-eyed, long-lashed child. Because she was born without a gallbladder, she was very ill and died just two years after her birth. When I see myself as this frail child, I feel deeply loved by my family. But I am also the source of great sadness to them in this brief, painful life. I start to cry as I see a tale of forgiveness weaving its way through my soul.

My grandmother suffered a great loss with the death of her youngest child. Just five years later, when I was born, Granny quickly chose me, her first grandchild, as her favorite. Although it may have been a healing situation for her, it caused great divisiveness in our family when my siblings were born shortly after me.

I was grateful for my grandmother's love, but I was defensive about it because her attitude caused my brother and sister to be resentful toward me. As other family members observed the favoritism, they entered the equation and began taking up sides. The tension was nearly constant. I used to wonder why my grandmother couldn't just love us three kids equally. I wanted my brother and sister to love me and for the entire family to be more peaceful. But, up to this point, I had not given much thought to my grandmother's perspective on the situation. And I had nearly forgotten about Beverly.

I had been trying to take a break from this past-life dance, but the music kept on playing. Had this vision of Beverly revealed another previous life as my aunt? All I can say with certainty is what it brought me, more compassion for a woman who deeply loved her last, lost child as well as her first grandchild. I became aware of my own lack of understanding, and I was willing to forgive my grandmother for her seemingly unfair treatment of us kids.

Annabelle. That was what the little angel guide had said her name was. It dawned on me that Anne was Beverly's middle name and my own as well. I knew that "belle" was the French word for beautiful. I had seen photographs of Beverly that revealed how beautiful she was. Maybe Annabelle was telling me that I was beautiful, too.

Chapter 8

$\mathcal{M}$Y RESEARCH REGARDING PERSEPHONE THE GREEK goddess led me to a book by Jean Shinoda Bolen, *Goddesses in Everywoman*, which gave me some startling information.

Persephone was a young maiden gathering flowers in a field when she was unwillingly abducted and raped by the god of the underworld, Hades. He took her to his kingdom to be his bride. The underworld symbolizes the unconscious, our dreams, spirituality, and mysticism. It can also represent the deeper layers of the psyche where memories have been buried (the collective unconscious). Darkness and depression, as well, are associated with the underworld.

I knew that just uncovering my repressed teenage assault wasn't enough. I needed to do some more processing. I thought back to my first dream, "The Beast at the Beach," in which a young man was terrorizing me with a weapon. At the time I missed what I now see was a sexual symbol. Because I did not get it at first, my inner wisdom brought the matter to my attention yet again.

My second dream, "An Obstacle in My Way," was more obvious. In it, I actually saw Greg, my old boyfriend. As I tried to greet him, a stern-looking, controlling woman tried to keep me away from him. She must have represented the fearful, frozen part of me that was protecting me from remembering the repressed rape. I was not healthy enough to deal with this traumatic incident earlier, so repression was my protection.

The dream woman's words were puzzling at first. "He didn't

recognize you." Later, I realized what they meant. My former boyfriend had not recognized me for who I truly was, a spiritual being worthy of respect and honor. Instead, he took advantage of me, violated me, and betrayed my trust. I was beginning to see how little I, too, had recognized and honored myself. I recalled my wise therapist asking me earlier if I had forgiven myself. A message from my higher self addressed this subject, too.

> h.s. You are stuck in your perceived guilt. I will tell you to let it go, to forgive yourself. This is what you absolutely need to do. But first, it may be necessary for you to let this awareness flood you in order to grasp the truth of your stuck position, to contemplate the enormous ramifications of how seeing yourself as guilty has kept you in chains.
>
> You are innocent, innocent, innocent.

There was an unusual twist in this drama about my ex-boyfriend that I realized offered me a unique opportunity on this healing journey. After he left my life and my hometown, he went on to achieve some national success with a weekly television program. It was shown in our Midwestern city at a very late hour. I had not set sight on him for many years. After I uncovered the repressed rape, I was curious how I might react to him. It dawned on me how simple it would be to find out. One evening, I decided to record his show.

The next day, I watched the tape. My response surprised me. Instead of being angry toward Greg, I seemed to be feeling little or nothing. I assumed there must be some anger in me, which needed to be expressed. So, I turned to my journal and began "telling him off." But it just didn't feel right. I had to admit that anger had been a very familiar feeling for most of my life. I wondered if I were still suppressing.

My reflections returned to the previous year. During that time,

I had seen a psychologist for rebirthing therapy. The ten lengthy sessions entailed continuous, deep breathing that induced a sort of altered state. This experience helped me get in touch with and express some intense feelings, especially anger. At the end of each session, I felt completely drained and quite peaceful.

I have often used anger as a defense or protection. It can be effective in holding someone at a distance when I felt too vulnerable for intimacy. The anger had somehow protected me from experiencing deeper, more painful feelings that I had not been willing or able to handle. Looking back, I see that the rebirthing experience was a good preparation for what inner work I would later do. It was necessary for me to release a lot of anger, which kept me from feeling the deep sadness I had buried. As I realized the hand of God on so many aspects of my life, I felt incredibly grateful.

When I looked back at what happened to me as a vulnerable young woman, I felt a deep sadness and disappointment. If only I had been able to fully express everything in my heart at the time I could probably have avoided a lot of pain later. But I just couldn't. At last, I could allow the feelings to emerge. Yes, it hurt. I did my best to treat myself with mercy.

> *h.s. There is so much sadness that has been bottled up in you, and it needs to come out. Let the tears flow. I love you. Please remind yourself often how very much you are loved. It is so hard for you to realize and to take it in. You long for things, people, and answers outside of you. It sometimes seems empty inside. But that is an illusion based on your past pain. Let the past go. It is forever gone. You are born again. It is a new world. You can love, and it can feel wonderful, not sad. Yet sadness can be a part—a small part—of your human existence. That is fine. Feel all your feelings. They are a part of you. You are a unique, valuable, beautiful part of me. You are a light. You need not be in darkness.*

I was led to tapes, readings, and meditations that enabled me to open more deeply to the sadness I had kept buried for so long. As I started to cry, it was sometimes difficult to stop. Sadness was not a feeling I eagerly embraced. However, it seemed to be a necessary part of my healing. There was a relief, a kind of cleansing effect that came from letting it out. Some of the sadness was about the rape. But there seemed to be other sorrows and disappointments I had been keeping locked inside me, which kept me from experiencing my life fully, the way I yearned to.

I found myself wondering about my former boyfriend. Where did he live now? Was he married? Had he taken responsibility for the rape? Had he forgiven himself? Or me? Did he feel I had ever hurt him? I knew I could wonder about him forever. But he alone was responsible for his own healing. I was the only one I could do anything about. So I had to continue working on my issues. I felt tense and agitated at my meditation period.

> *Dolfi comes to me on the beach, and I start to cry. "It's not safe being in this body," I say. "When did I first feel like this?" There's no response. Then I hear, "You are safe now." I begin to relax.*

I got another message and recorded it in my journal.

> *h.s. You are safe with me. I am your real self, your happy self, your wise, passionate, clear, godly self. You are so beautiful, precious, and good. Let go of the false, pleasing, angry, fearful self. She is nothing, a wisp of smoke. And yet you let her control you. You are free, the real you. You are safe. Rest, breathe deeply, and smile. You are free. You can be happy. Let go.*

I wanted to reach a sense of closure about the rape. I knew it could take a long time. But I had to at least start. I decided to write my former boyfriend a letter, though I knew I would not mail it. However, *A Course in Miracles* says that all minds are joined and we are not alone in experiencing the effects of our thoughts. So, I had a feeling that somehow the universe would convey my message.

> Dear Greg, Why did you hurt me? Didn't you know that I loved you? Maybe I hurt you, too. I forget. If so, I ask your forgiveness. I'm sorry. I couldn't love very well then. I was already wounded even before you hurt me. Did you know that? Maybe you were wounded, too. Maybe that's how we found each other, through our pain.
>
> Did you want to hurt me? I want you to know that you did. And what you did has stayed with me through all these years. Recently, I was reminded how much you meant to me and what you did to me. I am working on being healed. I am willing to forgive you completely. I love you and let you go with forgiveness.
>
> There were many reasons I blamed myself for what happened. I ask for the grace and mercy to forgive myself. I only wanted love from anyone in my life. I was in pain, and I wanted to be free. May I forgive myself completely and forever. May I see you and me with tenderness and loving kindness as the wounded children we were. May we both be free. Amen.

My daughter Rebecca, our oldest child, and I are very close. She has had her own path of healing. Some years ago, she told us that her father and I had fallen short as parents and gave us several examples. Her words saddened me. At first I felt defensive and guilty. Then I was guided to answer her honestly yet kindly.

"Honey, we did our very best," I said. "Certainly, we made mistakes, the same way our parents did with us. It's a difficult position.

I've been working on my issues for some time. Now that you're an adult, it may be time for you to do the same."

Rebecca did seek counseling at various times over the next few years. I am very proud of her for recognizing her need for help and obtaining it.

During this time of the dolphin, I started connecting some things I'd noticed earlier about our beautiful, bright daughter. She'd had a number of boyfriends over the years. And yet, she seemed at times to display a suspicious, even contemptuous attitude toward men. That troubled me. I usually attributed it to the strict, protective stance that her father took with his first and only daughter. But once the repressed rape surfaced in my consciousness, I realized that Becca may have been getting "beware of men" messages from me as well over the years. My cautions may have been largely on a subconscious level, yet they were real nonetheless. That must have made it difficult for her to trust men. I felt sad once I realized that and wanted to tell her of my awareness.

I had already told her tentatively about my dolphin spirit guide and what that meant. She is a creative, free thinker, too. And she didn't have to be told that her mom was a little out there. So, she listened to my mystical tale without scoffing. However, on a couple of occasions when I attempted to guide our conversation into a more personal area, she quickly retreated and changed the subject.

Then one day while driving her home from the airport, I realized she was a captive audience. I summoned my courage and blurted out my story of the date rape. I told her how I had repressed it and only recently became aware of its significance. I told her how it had traumatized me. I added that it may have subconsciously affected her, too. She listened attentively and responded with compassion.

Around that time, Becca met a young man who quickly became very important to her. I was delighted to notice a visible softening taking place in her as she so easily expressed her love and tender feelings for him. I wondered if she had just finally found the right guy. Or was there perhaps any connection between the opening I had recently allowed in my soul and the lovely blossoming of love in my daughter's world?

Chapter 9

WHILE PARTS OF MY SOUL WERE BEING LIFTED heavenward in my mystical adventures, dark and difficult vibrations were pulling another part of me downward.

One evening, Jonny came to us looking upset. He proceeded to unburden himself about his problems with gambling. I'd had some earlier suspicions about this possibility. I was upset, of course, but I was also somewhat relieved that he had brought this hidden vice out in the open. We told him he needed to see a therapist. He said he could handle it. I knew I could not make him heal from an addiction. But I wanted so badly to do something! My heart was breaking. We had already given him a deadline for leaving our home. I told him that, while he was still under our roof, he had to attend twelve-step meetings for gambling addiction.

My feelings toward our son were so complex. I loved him deeply. But I also felt sadness, fear, and, at times, anger toward him. Bright, sensitive, and funny, he attracted friends easily. But I saw him throwing away many of his God-given gifts, and that made me sad. I judged him as ungrateful to those who tried to help him and stupid for making such destructive choices. One day, at my meditation time, a revealing vision came to me.

> I see Dolfi lying on the beach on his back. His belly appears to have been cut open, and he is bleeding. "Dolfi, what happened?" I ask with concern. "Can I help you?"

He answers, "The only way you can heal me is by your forgiveness."

At once, I knew I had allowed myself to descend into the depths of blame and condemnation toward our son.

"Please, God," I cried, "soften my heart. Help me to forgive our son."

Dolfi, a symbol of my higher self, was prompting me, as Dr. Tom had earlier, to forgive myself. But my addictions (primarily codependency and control) caused me to focus first on others and ignore my own pain and responsibility.

As I was praying, a flood of darkness came upon me. I felt disturbing doubts and insecurities, questions of my own worth as a parent. I felt like I was drowning. Then grace intervened.

"Please, God," I finally pleaded, "teach me how to forgive myself."

As I wrote of my pain and my fear for Jon, I expressed the hopelessness I sometimes felt for him. I asked for guidance.

h.s. Do not be afraid. Heavenly beings protect you. Call light to you. Surround yourself with it. Lift yourself to the finer, higher vibrations of light and love. Do not be drawn downward to heaviness. Know this. You can do whatever you are called to do. You will be given the strength, courage, wisdom, patience, love, and determination to carry out any task that lifts you to your higher path.

My husband and I decided to seek help for ourselves. We attended twelve-step meetings for a while. It gave us good opportunities to share with others who had similar problematic situations. We would highly recommend Al-Anon or other such groups for providing experience, strength, and hope for such struggling families as our own.

After a restless, nearly sleepless night, I went to my meditation time and experienced great turbulence as a storm crashed in and over the ocean. I grabbed on to Dolfi's tail and took a wild, choppy, scary ride across the waves. I felt exhausted.

The anxiety that had plagued me for so long was increasing. I felt frustrated and impatient. I questioned why my body wasn't cooperating with me as I drew closer to my spiritual center. I was having frequent headaches, my back was hurting, and restful sleep often eluded me. When I woke up in the night, I occasionally took this quiet time to meditate or do some spiritual reading or writing. At one such session, I received this message:

> *h.s. Go slowly. Relax. You are on course. All is revealed in due time. You need not know everything at once. Love yourself. You are worthy of total love, just as you are, blemishes, insecurities, tensions, and all. Breathe deeply. Relax. Don't give up. There is nothing to give up but fear, and that is nothing. You are free at the core of you. It's just the outer edges that are caught and tied up.*

I had hoped to stay off medication, but I began thinking I needed to go back on it in order to function more fully. One day, I expressed my frustration at my increasing tension and the feelings of discouragement that were clouding my vision.

> *h.s. Embrace your humanness, your so-called weakness. As the Bible says, "My grace is sufficient for you, for my power is made perfect in weakness." What do you want to do? Levitate on a mountain? Then you'd be a great help to those around you! Instead, reach your head into the heavens and plant your feet firmly on the ground. This is the true glory of God, a person fully alive. Embrace the parts of you that you find un-embraceable. Love yourself. Forgive yourself. Be patient.*

This scriptural passage was one of my favorites. Recalling it helped calm me. Still, I decided I needed some help, so I made another appointment with my therapist.

Sometimes, I had read my journal messages to Dr. Tom. At first, I felt awkward and self-conscious in doing so. But it became easier.

"Do you know how blessed you are to be able to access your inner wisdom like that?" he said.

"Maybe I've begun taking it for granted," I replied. "I am gradually learning to trust my higher self and to acknowledge the truth that is so often reflected in these messages. But I wish I were better at remembering the words during difficult times and putting them into practice more faithfully."

"Don't go beating up on yourself," my therapist reminded me.

I told Dr. Tom that I was thinking of going back on antidepressants, even though I didn't want to.

"Why not" he asked. "You can take medication and still work on your issues."

Remember the side effects," I reminded him. Plus, I'm afraid the perfectionist part of me could judge myself a failure. And yet, because of the increasing anxiety, I am beginning to feel exhausted, as if I were treading water a good deal of the time, using all my faculties just to stay afloat. Any little thing seemed difficult, and problems like our son's gambling were nearly overwhelming.

Though we had pleaded with Jonathan to get help, he still thought he could handle things by himself. I brought my discouragement to my notebook pages and asked for help and insight. This is what I received.

> h.s. *Things need not always go smoothly in this sea of life. Sometimes, the waves roar, thunder crashes, and you think you'll drown, but you never do. It's all part of the plan.*
>
> *In the midst of the desert, water is within you. Don't let the apparent barrenness of the surrounding desert*

deceive you. But discipline is required until you have practice at finding the water's source. Know this: you are never alone. It only seems like that when you focus on the problems, the heat, and the seeming lack of abundance in this desert experience. Rich soil, rivers of water, trees heavy with fruit, and helpers too numerous to count fill the fields. But they must be seen with eyes of compassion, love, forgiveness, and gratitude as you walk amidst the seeming barrenness. Feel the cool breeze in the noonday desert heat. See the abundance in the stark landscape. This is the world of spirit that dances and thrives beneath the illusory world of form. You must learn the difference. You must experience the void before you can walk assuredly in the knowledge of the magnificence within and around you. You are not alone. You have been stumbling, but you do not have to fall. Walk slowly but mindfully with love as you continue on the journey.

Chapter 10

ONE DAY, MY HUSBAND SAW A BULLETIN BOARD NOTICE at work. A local support center for cancer patients was looking for volunteers. He signed up. I surprised myself by asking him to add my name to the list. It just felt right. And thus began my association with a wonderful organization to which I offered a small amount of time each week and received countless rewards.

I once read an interview with former First Lady Barbara Bush in which she was asked how she was able to deal with the untimely death of her young daughter many years earlier. She responded that volunteer work helped her to recover from the depression she was suffering due to this terrible tragedy. In the midst of my challenges over the years, I, too, have found that giving to others is a healing venture.

The Wellness Community provides educational and emotional support to cancer patients. I was immediately impressed with the caring, uplifting atmosphere I found there among the staff, volunteers, and participants. I assisted the staff in various ways: in the office, at workshops, at the front desk, or with the newsletter. The heroic way I saw others facing their life-threatening illnesses inspired me. If they could overcome, I knew I could, too, whether my challenges were emotional, physical, or spiritual.

Shortly after I began volunteering, I started wondering if, instead of donating my extra time, I should find a paying position. I felt a little guilty about not contributing to the family income even though we had no pressing needs at that time. The area of money has often been one in which my insecurities rise easily to the surface. Very soon, however, I had a vision, which I interpreted as encouragement to let go of my financial fears. It gently reassured me that I was in the right place at that time.

> *I am looking at the sky, which contains a beautiful rainbow arching the earth. Then I see Dolfi jump high and follow the stream of colors to its end, where there is the proverbial pot of gold. He picks up the treasure and brings it to me. He says that everything I could ever need is always available to me. I feel most grateful for all my blessings.*

One hot July afternoon, I was relaxing and reading in my comfortably cool family room. I was alone in the house, or so I thought. Then suddenly, I felt like someone else was there, too. I didn't see anyone, but I felt an intense physical presence. I was astonished to realize it was my father-in-law, who had passed away some seven years previously. Feelings of surprise and love erupted in me, and tears came to my eyes. I started a conversation in my mind.

"Dad, what are you doing here?" I asked.

There was no sense of a response. Still, my father-in-law's strong presence remained. I continued addressing him.

"Dad, I love you," I cried.

I gave him a spiritual hug and continued wondering why this was happening.

"You must know how concerned we are about Jonny. Could you please watch over him and, if you can, guide him?"

I pictured my father-in-law in my mind, remembering how he used to look. He was a big bear of a man with thinning gray hair, twinkling eyes, and a loving smile on his spectacled face. For a few brief, but lovely, minutes, I just relaxed and enjoyed his presence. But my logical, skeptical mind could not stay still for long.

I began thinking of other relatives and friends who were deceased. And then, a scary thought occurred to me. I recalled stories of people who seemed to see their departed loved ones right before they were about to die. I felt spooked!

Oh no, my thoughts said, arguing. *I'm not quite ready to depart the earth yet!*

And then, just as that fear began to wash over me, I realized my father-in-law's presence had vanished. In a little while, I resumed my household activities, but I still felt dazed. Why had this completely unexpected, most unusual visit taken place? Some ideas occurred to me.

I recalled how, during the last few months, I had tried to get my husband to join me in dieting. I would regularly remind him what he should and should not eat. Then I saw my father-in-law's face in my mind. I sensed him gently urging me to stop nagging his son, to just love him and let him be. And this awareness struck me. Our differences in form do not matter. Whether we are fat or thin, male or female, or tall or short is, ultimately, of no consequence. My father-in-law no longer even had a physical form. And yet, I was certain he had been right there in my family room with me.

What really mattered, I knew, was our essence. Spirit is who we truly are. I think that is what this kind, lovely man came to remind me that summer afternoon. His presence was also a confirmation of what I already believed. We do not really die or cease to exist. Instead, it is as if we merely enter another room, where our loved ones who are left behind cannot see us for a little while.

I told my husband and other members of his family about Dad's visit. My sister-in-law said that he had appeared to her about six months after he died. She had never mentioned this to me before. I suspect many people have such experiences, but they are reluctant to share them, for fear others might question their honesty or even their sanity.

Synchronicity greeted me in the mailbox one day. A five-week course, Mystical Awakenings, was being offered at a local college. I was naturally intrigued and curious to meet others whose inner travels might be even slightly similar to my own. I signed up.

The teacher was a mature, sophisticated, intelligent woman who had gone through some severe challenges, including a divorce from a long-term marriage and the onset of a seriously debilitating disease. She had been a lifelong churchgoer, but her traditional religious beliefs did not provide the answers and assistance she sought. In the midst of one dark, desperate night, she cried out for help and had an enlightening experience of spiritual ecstasy. It made her earthly problems pale by comparison. This mystical awakening assured her that she was not alone. Though she had previously considered ending her life, she was given the calm certainty that she could carry on with dignity and grace.

Our teacher directed us to writings about and by various mystics. She pointed out some of the common characteristics of their experiences. We meditated at every session and shared the unique way that Spirit was calling and leading each of us. One of the attendees had had a near-death experience. It gave her a spiritual assuredness, and it was the beginning of a series of psychic type occurrences. Another was having intense experiences of various types of energy in her daily life, which was challenging her. Each of us seven class members had our own story, but we were all there because of a deep inner desire for a different spirituality than what had been usually taught or acknowledged in most traditional religions. The class was fun and interesting. The universe had reminded me once more that I was definitely not alone on my spiritual journey.

The time for my next appointment with Dr. Tom arrived. I told him once again that I was losing interest in past lives. However, I decided to go ahead and try one last regression.

As usual, I found it hard to relax and get into the session.

After a while, I see Dolfi lying on the beach, and he tells me to "Let go." Next, I begin to describe an image that comes to me. I see a large church on the bluffs of a sea, a monastery.

Dr. Tom asked, "Can you go inside?"

I do that. I see myself as a monk. I am sitting before a large book, transcribing scripture passages. I try to uncover more of this image, but I am unsuccessful. I hear Dolfi telling me that I need to heal my relationship with the church.

I began to bring my awareness back to Dr. Tom's office. I related a recent, heated discussion about religion with a Catholic friend to the therapist. I thought about Dolfi's words, and I recognized the truth of what they were telling me. I knew I did not need to be affiliated with the church of my youth, but what I had to do for my own peace of soul was to forgive everyone and everything in my past, including the Church. It sounded like an overwhelming task, one that could take a lifetime. But then, what worthier goal could a lifetime have than forgiveness?

I told Dr. Tom about two past lives I had encountered during my meditation time. I recited them with a sense of detachment.

I am Henri, a painter in France. I have a wife, Angelique, and a daughter, Gisela, whom I care for. However, my art is so important to me that I often neglect my family …

…………………………..

> *I am a male artist, a sculptor, I think, somewhere in*
> *Eastern Europe. I am poor and live alone in a tiny room.*
> *Though I have few worldly possessions, I am very content*
> *and completely dedicated to my work. I think I am a*
> *homosexual.*

I did not feel very connected to these snippets of past lives. Perhaps they were just the result of an overactive imagination, or maybe I did actually live them in another time and place. Of course, I could not definitively answer that. Instead, I speculated as to their meaning. I knew I had always been, at the core, a very creative soul, and yet I had not nurtured that part of me until recently. In these two scenarios, my art was obviously an all-consuming passion, allowing time for little else. Had the karmic pendulum brought me to my current life in order to learn the great lessons inherent in human relationships? Could the single sculptor life explain my compassionate attitude toward homosexuals? I have often felt highly indignant when others make derogatory remarks about them. Well, I concluded these insights were interesting but not crucial.

A short time after this therapy appointment, I had yet another journey to the past at my meditation time.

> *I ask Dolfi to take me where I need to go. I find myself*
> *on a tropical island again. There is a great storm on the*
> *sea—darkness, wind, churning water, and fire from a*
> *far-off volcano. A tidal wave is occurring. I am terribly*
> *frightened, but despite my temptation to run away, I*
> *see myself yielding to the inevitable. The water begins to*
> *overtake me. Then I have a chilling awareness. In this*
> *life, I have a young child, whom I know is my older son*
> *in my present life. I begin to cry as I realize I cannot save*
> *him from the rising floodwaters. I struggle briefly, but I*
> *feel so powerless, inadequate, and guilty. A part of me*
> *knows what I must do—let him go. My guides are there.*

*They tell me all is well. I must trust. I start to relax, to let
go, to let my son go. I allow peace to overtake me. I feel
water filling my lungs. Then the turmoil is gone. There is
peace. I feel grateful. As I rise above the chaos, I look to
where the island had been. It is gone. I understand that
it was merely the stage where an important drama has
played out. I get in touch with some remaining feelings
of guilt about not being able to save my small son from
the tidal wave disaster. I start to cry.*

I could feel the echoes of this scene reverberating through the
years and spilling over into my current life. My prayer was that I would
someday be able to accomplish what this vision had told me I must.

Chapter 11

*F*EELINGS WERE CAUSING ME SOME MORE PROBLEMS. FOR a while after I had discovered the past-life harem scenario, I thought my infatuation toward my therapist was resolved. But then I recognized some of those old lovesick feelings emerging again. I suspected that my longtime habit of repression had probably been at work.

I began noticing how very much I tried to be in control of what I said and even felt during my sessions with Dr. Tom. If a loving feeling arose, I usually managed to quickly suffocate it. It felt embarrassing, and I didn't know how to deal with it. In my quiet, introspective times at home, if such feelings came up, I just did my best to repress them by focusing on something else. I wanted so badly for this whole issue to go away. Books had told me that transference was a normal, healthy part of the psychotherapeutic process. I understood intellectually that my therapist was serving as some kind of symbol to me. But my head and my heart were worlds apart.

Early in the therapy, I had asked Dr. Tom in a teasing way, "How do you feel about being a sex symbol?"

He raised his eyebrows and shoulders, grinned broadly, and exclaimed laughingly, "Who me? What can I say?"

I later thought how adorable he was at that moment. I wished he were ugly and stupid and would do something to make me hate him. But I knew he wouldn't. I had put him on a pedestal, and from my distant view below, he looked just perfect. The harder I resisted these adoring feelings, the more they persisted.

I used to think that I was a very honest person. I tried to be. But as this process of therapy shone a spotlight on my feelings and behavior, I discovered how often I fell short of complete honesty, especially with myself. When I noticed how uncomfortable I sometimes felt during sessions, I asked, "Why?" The truth was that I wanted so much for this person to like me. Then I reminded myself that I was just one of his many clients. And I mentally listed all the reasons why he could not possibly like me. I was neurotic, I said stupid things, I was old, and I was no longer attractive...etcetera, etcetera... Such thoughts made my body tense up and my stomach tighten.

Then when I was outside of the therapist's office, I started to tune into myself and recognize how I felt around others. At a wedding, for example, when I checked my body, I could feel my stomach and shoulders tightening at times. At one of my group meetings, when it was my turn to speak, I became aware that a smile was frozen on my face and my fists were clenched. Sometimes when I listened, I could hear myself playing word games, trying to display my verbal facility, telling interesting stories, and hoping to impress others or make them laugh. I had to conclude that it wasn't only Dr. Tom I was trying to impress. It was pretty much everybody. Trying to be accepted by others when I hadn't accepted much about myself was exhausting.

For most of my life, crying did not come easily to me. I had kept a tight lid on my feelings. Maybe I was afraid that, if I ever started, the tears might never stop. But I was beginning to break through some of those fearful barriers. The tears had begun. I didn't know when they'd end. I supposed when I was ready. At first, I thought the sadness was due to my recognition of the repressed rape. Then I blamed my attachment to my therapist. I began to see that the tears were releasing even more. I wrote in my journal about years of longing to feel loved while feeling unlovable. I said I felt tightly wrapped up in a tiny ball, unable to give love completely to anyone in my life, most especially myself. This response came.

h.s. Tap the wellsprings of feelings that run so deep within you. Use this energy to bless, to forgive, and to heal. You are not lukewarm. But you have allowed yourself to think that you are. You couldn't allow yourself to feel the intensity of your emotions, and so you repressed, denied, and closed down. But though it hurts for a while, this is a time of release, of healing. The windows of your soul are opening. Light is pouring out. It hurts because it's been bottled up for so long, but soon you will feel. You have already felt it a little. It's freer than you've ever known. Just let the feelings come. Let the tears flow. Allow grace to touch every pore and to fill every cell. My vessels are purified. It must be so. You are my vessel. I love you. Never forget this.

Once I began tapping into more of my feelings and was able to cry easily and frequently, my husband became disturbed. The anger I had sometimes displayed to keep away my sadness had, of course, been troubling to him. But he did not find my frequent tears a great improvement. His typical male pattern of wanting to fix me or make me better was frustrating. I just wanted him to tell me what I was trying to tell myself, that it was okay for me to feel my feelings. I wanted to know he was there for me. But I knew, too, what was most important was learning how to be there for myself. I tried to explain to him how beneficial it was for me to express my sadness. I also had to withdraw to my room at times where I could feel my feelings freely, not worrying how it was affecting someone else.

My life was full, and there was much to be grateful for. Still, I felt stuck at times, struggling with ever-present challenges in my various roles as mother, wife, daughter, sister, and friend. I continued to explore inner worlds, yet I felt hesitant and even fearful sometimes of what I might find. In my journal, I wrote, "Dear Father/Mother God, I love you. I am grateful for the perfection of this moment for the strength you give me. Walk with me. I yield to my higher wisdom's response."

h.s. Yes, I walk with you always. Do not be afraid, though you are sorely tempted to do so nearly every moment. It has been your way of life. But there is a way out. You are seeing the light beginning to shine and flutter through the deep thicket of trees in the forest of your doubts and fears. Concentrate only on that light. See it, appreciate it, and focus on it until it grows and penetrates every corner of your darkest places. You are that light. Do not let fear of anything obscure it. Do not be afraid of the fear. Nothing will harm you. Look at it, and see how unworthy of respect all fears are. Simply see it, and lay it aside. Embrace your dear self, who is so unable to see her light and her beauty that she has felt forced to hang on to these silly shadows for support. Let everything go but the light, and you are free.

I was thinking less and less about past lives. I had a hard time deciding whether I believed in reincarnation or not. I just felt caught up in my life now and didn't seem to have the time, energy, or desire to focus on then. And yet, the issue still came up at times, usually when I was least expecting it. One day, a theme I had contemplated before returned in my reading, "embracing the un-embraceable," as a necessary part of moving to a higher path. I wrote about it in my journal and pondered a while before moving into my meditation. An unexpected scenario emerged. First, I'll provide some background.

My husband had a younger brother who was diagnosed as a child with paranoid schizophrenia in early adolescence. Needless to say, he had a difficult life. So did his entire family as they struggled to cope with this bewildering affliction. From the first time I met my future brother-in-law Gary when he was about sixteen years old, I felt very uneasy around him. He was often in his own world, muttering to himself and displaying odd, inappropriate actions and feelings. This strange behavior repulsed and frightened me.

In the meditation, as I was thinking about embracing the

unembraceable, Gary suddenly appeared in my mind. The thought arose that our soul somehow chooses the part we will play in this drama of life. If that were so, it seemed that Gary had taken on a very difficult task. He presented a challenge to many of us whose lives he had touched. It was not easy to love this person in such an unpleasant form. Never before had it occurred to me what courage was required by my brother-in-law to tackle such a demanding role.

And then in my mind, like a multilayered dream where one thing becomes another, I saw my younger son, Drew, who was tall, handsome, bright, and funny. The love I felt for him brought a smile to my heart. This thought followed, "Gary and Drew are one." I wondered if this referred to reincarnation.

My poor, tormented brother-in-law had such a hard time fitting into the normal world. At the age of twenty-two, he took his own life. This was approximately seven years before Drew was born. So, it was possible, if reincarnation actually occurred, that Gary's soul could indeed have reincarnated as our son. The idea was shocking. I tried to understand it logically, but of course, I couldn't.

I knew that my mind was not where I needed to be to embrace my deceased brother-in-law. My lofty mountain of mental imaginings is where I often retreat in order to avoid feeling something that might be too painful. Just one step, I knew, could take me to the place where true healing happens, but it can sometimes be a long trip. I thought of Gary and then of Drew. One? I asked for help, and then I waited. Soon, the tears began.

"Oh, Gary, I'm so sorry," I cried. "Please forgive me." Tears rolled down my cheeks.

I did it. I took the giant leap from my head into my heart. The view from there was astounding. At that moment, I could see so clearly. Each of us is Spirit. No one is higher; no one is lower. We are each united with one another in perfect equality. And so indeed, we all are one.

Chapter 12

THE HOUSE WHERE WE LIVED DURING THIS TIME OF THE dolphin had a huge deck that overlooked lots of trees. I enjoyed relaxing there, meditating, writing, and getting in touch with the wonders within. As a true introvert, this was where I usually hung out. I had paid little attention to the enormous beauty outside me. But that was about to change.

My Monday night study group had introduced me to Ken Carey's intriguing, inspiring books several years earlier. Carey, born in Chicago, realized his dream of owning a large plot of land in the foothills of the Ozark Mountains in southern Missouri. As he and his wife raised a family in this primitive place with few modern conveniences, Carey got deeply in touch with the rhythms of nature. In the quiet, he began hearing otherworldly messages. Fortunately, he wrote them down. I had read a number of his mystically beautiful books.

At the library one hot summer day, I was excited to see a new title by Ken Carey, *Flatrock Journal*. Thinking it was like his other volumes, I checked it out. I was surprised to find it was instead a description of life on his eighty acres in the Greenwood Forest. It did not take long for me to become entranced. Carey's writing is exquisite, and his love of the land shone clearly on each page of this book. I began to fall in love.

Our development was bursting with huge trees, lush plants, colorful, lyrical birds, playful squirrels, and a lake that shimmered with the morning sun and glimmered in the moonlight. But I had hardly noticed any of it! As my eyes and ears began to open, so did my heart. I was grateful for this master storyteller who awakened me to yet another part of my world. My meditations became even more meaningful as I sat outside and really saw the grandeur around me even as the beauty within bubbled forth. One day, while sitting on the deck, I became inspired with a feeling of intense peace. I received these words and wrote them in my journal.

> *h.s. Now you're getting it! Peace is in every breath you take if you but let go and let the world and the universe support you. Doesn't it feel good to do this? Aren't the heavenly arms that support, encircle, and embrace you enough to let you feel loved and blessed?*
>
> *Flow gently with the stream of life. See the beauty at every turn, and feel the happy heart of gladness that beats within you when you are listening to the heavenly harmony that resonates within and around you. There is no difference—no separation—between you and the sunset, the rain, the lightning, the butterfly, the rose, and the sweet sounds of violins and harps that hint of heaven's eternal harmonious symphonies. All you need to grasp is a hint here and a flicker there, and soon you will be able to tune in more frequently to the love and peace that is always here and there, but you have blocked from fear, anxiety, and habits that hamper your vision. Though you are blind, you have unseen helpers that are leading you through heavenly places. Open your eyes now and then. The beauty is intoxicating and healing. Let go.*

We'd had a vacation in Phoenix early in June. It was delightful getting reacquainted with friends we'd made during our years of living there. I was pleased to find how receptive and affirming our friends were when I shared some of my mystical Dolfi experiences.

Then early in July, some Midwest friends offered us a week in Wisconsin with them. One cool July morning, I sat by the lake and tried to meditate and relax. These suggestions came.

> *h.s. Simply be. You need do nothing. You need not plan, think, tend to, take care of, worry, or work. Let the peace of divine holiness permeate your being. Let it wash over you, and let it refresh and pacify you. Learn how to love yourself, and that peace will flow over to everyone. Let everything go. Stop clinging to being right or wrong, feeling hurt, wanting something else, regretting, or having unforgiveness or anything that is not you—pure love, forgiveness, and joy. You deserve to be loved, happy, and free. You deserve all good, for that is the core of who you are. Throw away the excess baggage. Whenever you feel heavy, just say, "I'm going to let go of this heavy load that binds me," and mentally picture yourself untying a huge rock that was strapped on your back. Soon you will feel lighter and freer than ever, and your burden will lessen.*

I longed to feel light and free. And I succeeded at times. But that persistent visitor, anxiety, was still hanging around. While on vacation, I decided to resume taking the antidepressant I had not taken for some time. It wasn't logical, but I felt a little disappointed in myself. I wished I were stronger, calmer, and healthier. I wished I were perfect. But what I needed was relief.

Not long after we returned from our trip, I began preparations for an upcoming weekend during which we were hosting several couples at our home. I was uptight about all that needed to get done. I felt burdened and asked for help with my negative attitude.

> *h.s. Be grateful for the great blessing you have in friends. Relax. Enjoy. Take frequent rests, and get in touch with*

*me. Let go of all unnecessary concerns, fears, and worries.
Because they are all unnecessary, you are then free. Love
yourself, your family, and all the opportunities presented
to you daily to love. Remember the wrong turn you made
on your trip? You were frustrated and upset at this
mistake. And what did it do? It gave you an opportunity
to see some beautiful scenery and ultimately to end up at
a different place at a different time, one precisely right
for you. What did you lose? Thirty minutes? What is
time? With me, there is no time. Heaven is now and
timeless. Time is only for your learning. Remember, not
your enemy but your friend will help teach you to let go,
let it be, and love.*

These words helped, and yet during the weekend, I got caught up
in things to do and didn't take time to rest and to pray. I started to
feel frazzled.

Why did I expect so much of myself? I thought, wondering to myself.

I found myself focusing on petty, little differences between the
others and me. I got up early Sunday morning, sat on my deck, and
prayed for help.

*h.s. God's plan is to walk in the light, not in the shadows.
God's plan is to love yourself as I love you. God's plan is to
see the real you, Spirit, and to see others the same way. Do
not focus on extraneous, unimportant differences. God's
plan is to do your being, letting your natural talents flow
and create and produce. The ego wants to separate; God
wants to unite. The ego wants to blame; God wants to
forgive. The ego hates; God loves. The ego criticizes; God
appreciates. Salvation is peace, happiness, light, and
love, all that is good. Why would you waste your time
and effort with anything else? God's plan of forgiveness
gives you all you could want. Why go elsewhere? Go*

to forgiveness. Bless everyone and everything and first
yourself with forgiveness, and you will be free.

These good thoughts calmed me down and lifted me up. The day went beautifully, and the weekend was overall successful.

In addition to the wisdom I received from my internal teacher were great blessings of insight that came from the many books I regularly embraced. Jean Jensen in *Reclaiming Your Life* suggested becoming keenly aware when we are stuck in painful patterns of uncomfortable feelings and unproductive patterns. At such times, Jensen says we can learn how we are often repeating unresolved issues from our childhood. I began trying some of her exercises.

When I got upset with my husband, children, or someone else (myself included), I retreated to my quiet place and closed the door. Then I worked on returning in my mind and spirit to a time earlier. I became a little child, as Dolfi had earlier suggested. Indeed, I found I was often replaying earlier issues I had not yet resolved, like loneliness, helplessness, and feelings of abandonment. It helped to recognize what was really going on. This kind of inner work was hard, but I felt hopeful that these kinds of technique could contribute much to my inner healing.

In one of my journal entries, I was cautioned to not be caught up in illusions.

Then at my next appointment, Dr. Tom said, "You're taking this life thing too seriously. Don't you know it's an illusion?"

This made me smile and gave me reason to reflect. *A Course in Miracles* frequently refers to this world's illusionary aspects. But I so often act like my problems are damned important, that is, real! Sure, my challenges can feel painful. And I felt certain this inner work of mine was important. But I was also learning to listen. Maybe I needed to take heed of what the universe seemed to be telling me. Maybe I needed to lighten up and take a break!

I wondered how long it had been since I'd relaxed with a good novel. I even get a kick out of the trashy tabloids with their bizarre gossip now and then. Maybe it was time for me to put on my serious shopping shoes and spend a day or two in hypnosis at the mall. Or swinging by Blockbuster to rent a stack of old Woody Allen or Steve Martin DVDs sounded terrific, too.

Anything can be addictive, including therapy, meditation, self-analysis, or reading. Balance is an important of mental, emotional, and spiritual health. Yes, I was grateful for this important reminder. On a regular basis, I needed to get serious about having some fun!

Chapter 13

*M*Y JOURNALS WERE FILLING WITH NOTES, MESSAGES, prayers, dreams, joys, and struggles as my journey continued. Now and then, I reread them and continued to be amazed. For a while, I had thought that my Dolfi was something or someone separate from me. I gradually came to see him as a symbol of my higher self. Along the way, however, I was drawn to several nonfiction books on dolphins, which gave me reason to ponder many new ideas. These books speak of a deeply personal, powerful, intense connection that the dolphins as a species are making with their human friends on our planet. That confirmed that my experiences were not as rare as I'd once thought.

Is it possible that a dolphin consciousness could somehow break into our human world and give rise to such visions, dreams, and inspiring words as those I have received? Such a concept is beyond my intellectual understanding. What I do know is that I have experienced some amazingly beautiful gifts from the presence of my Dolfi, and for that, I am grateful. And yet, at this point in time, I have had to conclude that the source of my inspiring words was an aspect of my self. That self is greater and wiser than the little personality me but, nonetheless, as much a part of me as my heartbeat

My writing practice has been, at times, my anchor, therapist, friend, mother to my inner child, comforter, and guide. Usually, the inner stirrings would come during my quiet times. But, now and then, I found the familiar heart sounds in the midst of people or activity.

KATHY SCHMIDT

Then, if possible, I tried to pull away, get my paper and pen, and record what I heard.

As I became more comfortable with yielding to these inner messages, they grew longer. The words sometimes rushed so quickly that I could not sense their meaning as I wrote. Then, when I reread what my hand had recorded, I was often surprised and grateful. At times, I felt humbled even to tears to see the beauty of what had come through me. By myself, I didn't think I could have written much of this material. I needed Spirit's inspiration. Step by step, I was learning to trust. My greatest challenge was putting into practice what my inner wisdom told me.

One day in my meditation period, I began thinking about my therapist. Those troubling, adoring feelings arose, followed quickly by sadness. I realized how much I'd been avoiding this issue. Something had to be done about it. I decided to face the matter head-on in my next therapy session. I knew this was important. But it was embarrassing and would require making myself very vulnerable. I knew this transference thing was supposed to be a positive part of therapy. And I reminded myself that feelings were neither right nor wrong. They just were.

This therapy process was so intriguing, a microcosm of my entire life. I brought all the problems that I experienced outside Dr. Tom's office to our counseling sessions. This included issues like my fragile self-esteem, fear of intimacy, lack of trust, as well as challenges and blocks of all kinds. A fairly recent subject I had been grappling with was that of aging.

I had actually found these midlife years were, for the most part, positive. I was getting more in touch with the real me that had remained hidden for so long. I remembered chuckling inwardly as I watched older friends going through struggles with their maturity. As I scrutinized the subject from a younger viewpoint, I thought I was more enlightened than they were. I did, after all, have a huge celebration to honor myself by achieving my fiftieth birthday. Well, that was then. And this is now.

Facial lines were deepening, anatomy parts drooped, and my waistline was fading. It happened very slowly of course. But some days, as I looked in the mirror and saw a stranger gazing back, it seemed to have occurred overnight. I felt certain I appeared old to others, including my therapist, who was eight years younger. I was becoming painfully aware of my every flaw that resulted from this tyranny of time. Throughout my life, I had often lacked self-confidence, but I still recalled a time not too long ago when I used to feel at least reasonably attractive. Again, that was then.

I also struggled with trust. I remembered how Dr. Tom told me early on, "You're safe with me." Being able to trust him was most important as I began to plunge into the icy waters of self-revelation. I recognized how little I had trusted others. This process seemed to require that he trusted me, too. I was annoyed at first when I noticed his reluctance to give me direct advice. Instead, he would ask, "How do you feel about it?" or "What do you think?" Unfortunately, I was more comfortable with being told what I should feel or think. I'd had so little practice getting in touch with my desires and needs that it was hard to answer his questions. But I was starting to see that his trust in my ability to find my own way was an important part of this healing process.

At my next session, I got up the courage to tell Dr. Tom that I was still experiencing those adoring feelings toward him despite my efforts to repress them. I felt awkward talking about it. He didn't seem shocked or surprised. (I wondered if he heard this often from his clients. Did many of them become infatuated with him? What a job!) He repeated what he had said earlier, that is, I needed to work through this issue. But if it were too much of a stumbling block, he would have to refer me to another therapist. Then there was silence.

Okay, I thought. *I could handle that. It made sense.*

I would see another shrink if that's what it took to lessen my struggles with life. I wanted to be happy more often. I still wasn't sure what this "working through the transference" meant exactly, but I supposed I'd find out. When I came into this session, I felt vulnerable, embarrassed, and afraid of appearing foolish. But afterward, I felt relieved and even empowered. It felt good knowing I had the courage to bring my issues, especially the painful ones, out in the open. That was the only place where I could see what was going on. I was learning not to run away from my feelings.

I was experiencing less anxiety as a result of returning to the medication. But there was a price. I had less urgency to pursue my visualization experiences. When they did occur, they were usually smaller and quieter. I was less able to tap into my dreams, too. I suppose I could say I was more laid back. Actually, in a way, I felt relieved to reduce my intensity of recent times. Low gear was sounding comfortable for a while. But there were still great rewards from an ongoing meditation practice when I took time to be quiet and bring what was within me to the surface, both positive and negative.

I am in a beautiful autumn forest. Colorful leaves cover the ground. I see a huge oak tree before me. Nestled at its base is a small, white lamb. I realize that both the tree and the lamb represent aspects of me. I see myself as strong and powerful as the oak, able to withstand great storms and vastly changing conditions. Like the lamb, I also embody tender, sweet qualities such as gentleness and innocence.

This vision helped me reflect on my goodness, my positive qualities. Affirmations are a wonderful way of building self-esteem. Positive, uplifting thoughts and words that remind me of my great worth are extremely healing. I must remind myself regularly what a gift I am to the universe. The world may call this egotistical. But Spirit, I believe, would call it truth.

"I am strong, gifted, and holy. My life is purposeful, rich, beautiful, and good. I am one with God. I am a powerful person. I am free. The universe is filled with blessings at my disposal. I love who I am and all

I do. God loves me completely. I am God's beloved child. I am healing. I receive all I need. I am holy."

Autumn is a lovely season in the Midwest. Our older son, Jonny, had been transferred to another city. I prayed he would be fine, but I still felt concern for him. Our younger son, Drew, was back in school. Our daughter was in love. My husband Ted was on a work project that involved seven Russian engineers who had traveled here from their homes across the globe. Toward the end of this one-month project, there was a social event with the local employees of Ted's company and their families, as well as the foreign visitors.

It was a beautiful Saturday afternoon at a local winery with the trees arrayed in their autumn colors and the air cool and crisp. Blankets were spread on a hill with a breathtaking view of the valley below. Americans and Russians alike nibbled our snacks and sipped our wine. Here we gathered, people from worlds once steeped in hatred and mistrust of one another were now talking and laughing with the aid of interpreters. Yesterday, they worked together. Today, we joined in play. Both occupations transcended politics and language. The peace and unity I witnessed that afternoon was inspiring. For more than six months, I had been focusing intently on my own individual healing. This afternoon, I felt extremely grateful to glimpse a tiny spark of the great miracle of peace that was catching fire around the world.

Slowly, the sun began slipping over the horizon. As darkness fell, a chill crept into the air. Winter was coming.

Chapter 14

ONE DAY AFTER A TROUBLING TELEPHONE CONVERSATION with my mother, old feelings flooded and upset me. Later, I yelled at my husband and son. I felt stuck in an emotional revolving door with no escape. It was, unfortunately, a familiar scenario. I knew I needed help. I went to my room and locked the door.

> *I get in touch with my inner child. She is feeling so powerless. I see myself hollering at my mommy. I tell her how mad she is making me and how bad I feel. Then I take a deep breath and try to go deeper, beneath the anger.*

I started to cry. I picked up my journal and wrote how sad, lonely, and lost my little child is feeling. I ask for guidance.

> *h.s. Cry and cry some more. It is good to do this. You are loved. Your mother was and is in such pain. That's all she knows. That's all you knew, too, but you are healing. You can get beneath the surface, get to the core, and be healed. Let yourself be healed. Be still and let Spirit heal you.*

As I worked on getting in touch with my little inner child, I gained some clarity about my attachment to my therapist. The logical, adult part of me could see how inappropriate these schoolgirl feelings were. I knew that Dr. Tom was a very nice but normal person with his own problems, not some perfect being. But my little wounded girl inside had been longing for love for a long time, and she had idealized him.

Little Kathy could not interpret her mommy's raging and blame as merely symptoms of her own deep pain. Instead, she felt rejected. My little child did not understand why Mommy was always tending to her younger siblings while expecting such mature behavior from her, even though she was barely older than them. She felt alone and abandoned.

I wish she would love me, she thought. *I guess I'm not good enough.*

She wondered why her brother and sister were resentful toward her. She couldn't help it that she was Granny's favorite. And she certainly did not want to be the perfect one or the family hero, a role she somehow got hooked into playing.

I wish they would love me. I guess I'm unlovable, she thought.

As I grew up, my inner child yearned for love from others, too. As a teenager, I had thought Greg loved me until I learned how unloving he had treated me. After that, I must have been too scared to let those longing for love feelings to emerge. I was so afraid of rejection that I usually repressed my feelings. Sometimes, I used anger to avoid intimacy. That was easier than feeling the sadness underneath my feelings of unworthiness. Then I found a safe place with my therapist. My little child saw him as wise, kind, accepting, and aware enough to understand her pain. My repressed yearning to love and be loved began to emerge. And I transferred them to Dr. Tom.

Okay, I was starting to "get it," intellectually speaking. But my heart hadn't caught up yet with my head. My feelings were not so easily translated to logic and psychological terms. I felt like I was caught up in a real-life soap opera. When I detached and watched this story from afar, I told myself to "get it together" and stop being so sappy. But when I got back inside my own skin, my longing to be loved but feeling unlovable was very real, and it hurt.

For several nights, I slept fitfully. Early the next morning, I grabbed a jacket and went outside to sit on my deck. The cool, crisp air announced the coming cold front. Scattered leaves with hints of color clung stubbornly to the nearly stark tree branches. Squirrels frolicked amidst the sea of brown foliage that covered the ground. I felt tired and headachy. Something told me, "Don't push the pain away." I closed my eyes, took a couple of deep breaths, and tried to embrace it, to hear what it had to say. I was amazed to learn how very wise that nasty headache was.

> h.s. Stop demanding so much of yourself. Just relax and enjoy the beautiful day Stop worrying and fretting about so many unimportant details of the illusion.

The adult me mentally picked up my little child and held her tenderly in my arms. I told her how much I loved her. I realized how lost that dear little one had been feeling. I started to cry.

I prayed, "Teach me how to love myself."

My two guides, the dove and Persephone, had pretty much faded from my consciousness. Dolfi remained, however, sort of like a guardian angel that I called on at times. I was still meditating, but the visualizations I used to have regularly now occurred only occasionally. At times, though, they were especially affirming.

> I see the Grand Canyon, a breathtaking, magnificent, sweeping panorama. Many tourists are gathered around its rim, admiring the beauty. Then I see at, in its midst, a tiny speck of light at the very bottom of the canyon. The speck starts growing gradually larger until it becomes a great light that illuminates the whole landscape. Suddenly, I am astonished to realize that the light is me. Then I hear these words, "I am the light of the world."

The holidays were approaching. This time of year was a challenge for me. Spirit gave me some good thoughts to ponder.

h.s. Don't get caught in the holiday illusions of the world. If you wish to participate in the game, do so. Just remember. In its midst, you can and must remember what is important: love, peace, and forgiveness. That is all.

I was close to the end of my insurance company's allotted therapy sessions with Dr. Tom. I could have asked him, I suppose, if he suggested further treatment, but frankly, I felt "therapied" out. During this process, I had discovered much about myself. I even made some significant breakthroughs. I was grateful that panic attacks had not troubled me in quite a while. And yet, there were still times when I felt emotionally like I was at square one. I yearned to be on a path that progressed continually forward. Mine was more like three steps forward and then two back. During those backsliding periods, I could get pretty discouraged.

Because it was almost the end of the year, I let the calendar help determine the demise of this therapy. I did wonder if I had become too dependent on Dr. Tom. If a crisis came up, would I be strong enough to handle it without his support and guidance? In one of my last sessions, I told him that I was still not over him and it bothered me. As usual, he was fairly noncommittal, and that was annoying. I had to remind myself that I needed to find my own answers. I still was somewhat uncertain about this reincarnation thing that I had begun what seemed like a long time ago. What was I missing? I felt powerless and tearful. But then I allowed myself to relax and told myself that I didn't need to figure it all out. Maybe I could just accept things the way they were. I picked up my journal to record this message:

h.s. Love is indeed a raging river, a force to move mountains, to move worlds. Experience its power. Let it teach you, not overwhelm you. Kneel in its presence. Respect the power, the strength, of love. This is only a speck compared to the Love that loves you, encircles you in its arms, gives you every breath, pumps each drop of blood throughout your body, holds you to its bosom, and never ever lets you go. Imagine the Love that pulsates throughout the universe, the one that speaks worlds into existence and never leaves you. This you must remember—often, daily, and hourly—the fierceness of Love with which you are loved. Remember, and be still and be healed.

I continued volunteering weekly at the Wellness Community. Many of the programs there were geared toward relieving stress in the cancer patients, enabling their immune systems to function better. One of the more popular workshops was Creative Visualization, which was much like my own personal meditative experiences. As a volunteer assistant, I was invited to join the sessions along with the cancer patients. The psychologist first suggested that the participants breathe deeply and get relaxed. Then she encouraged everyone to allow inner images to emerge. We were to inwardly verbalize what we saw. This process continued for a while, ten minutes or so. Then she urged us to gently bring our awareness back to the room, counting backward before we opened our eyes. We were then encouraged to share what we received and discuss what we thought the images meant.

During a workshop one afternoon, I was gifted with this lovely scenario.

I see a woman wearing a bonnet working in a garden. The sun is shining, and a swarm of black birds is flying in the sky. One of the birds leaves the others and sits on a fence near the woman. Then the sky clouds up, and it starts to rain. The bird begins to worry about the woman as she watches her go into the house. The other birds call to their friend on the fence to join them in flying south. She is reluctant to go because of her anxiety about the woman, but she knows she must leave. The black bird begins to fly straight up, high into the sky. Suddenly, she undergoes a transformation and becomes an eagle. The rain stops, and the sun begins to shine.

The woman in the garden and the bird both seemed to be aspects of myself. The woman's work in her garden was my inner healing journey. The black bird was the fearful part of me who worried about leaving that work with the therapist. Other birds (fears) invited that part of me to join them. But I had the courage to stay on the path, to let go of my fears. As I flew upward (moving toward God), I was transformed into my higher self (eagle). I saw that the real me was powerful, and I was free.

At my last therapy session in this Year of the Dolphin, we looked back at where I'd been some nine months earlier and where I was at that moment. We agreed that I had made progress. It had helped me believe that I could trust Dr. Tom and he could help me. Perhaps it also showed me that I could always, as *A Course in Miracles* advises, "Choose again if a decision was made unwisely in the past." I could choose only love now for my therapist, whereas in the former life, it seemed that I chose obsession and despair about a similar attraction.

The subject of medication came up. A couple of months earlier, I had told Dr. Tom that I guessed I'd always have to take medicine for depression.

"Why?" he asked simply.

I posed the same question to myself and began reexamining that issue. It was to be an ongoing challenge, but I was coming to some peace about it. I was learning that whether or not to take medication was not the problem. I needed to ask myself frequently, "How can I best love myself?" My answer may differ at times. I need to regularly review and be flexible and open in making such a decision.

I was learning that anxiety and depression often resulted from deep issues, some of which I may not be ready to look at. Healing cannot be rushed. It may take time. I need to love myself even when I am not ready to get out of denial or deal with a particular matter.

I can use medication at times when it is necessary or helpful. The *Course in Miracles* refers to medicine as "magic," that is, something that works on the surface, or symptoms of illness, not at its source. But sometimes, a little magic may be the best way for me to love myself.

Dr. Tom told me that he was there if ever I needed him, and that felt reassuring. One of the last inner messages I received that year was this:

> *h.s. There is never ever any need for fear. I am with you always. I am enough. You are enough. You've done the work. You have remained on the path, though you were tempted to go astray. You remain faithful, and you are at peace. That peace will always be the indicator that you are on track. Do not worry. Only trust. Know you are safe and cared for and you can fly high above the illusions, the rain, and the darkness of this world. You can be an eagle soaring in the sunny skies so high. Be still, and know it is so.*

Part 2

Back on the Road to Recovery

Chapter 15

SHORTLY AFTER CHRISTMAS, JONATHAN CALLED TO SAY that he had lost his entire paycheck gambling and could not pay his rent. He asked if we would lend him some money. Ted said no, and I agreed with him. But my feelings fought with my logic. In anguish and tears, I went to my journal.

> h.s. Crying is a release. It is good to release pent-up feelings. You love him, and you are hurting. But know this: you need not worry. Worry accomplishes nothing. Trust, trust, trust. Put all your trust in the divine to resolve everything ultimately for the good. God's Word is always good. God loves Jon. Eternal forgiveness, blessing, goodness, guidance, mercy, and help are always available to everyone. Know that all things work together for good. This will pass. If your son chooses pain, that is his choice, as it has been yours in the past. Let him and the situation go.

A week later, I picked up a premonition and suggested we call Jonny. Sadly, my fearful intuition was correct. He had just been fired from his job, so he was without a job, car, or money in a city where he knew nearly no one. I felt sad and helpless. I wanted so badly to do something. Ted agreed to see Dr. Tom with me. We poured out our pain to the therapist. He listened compassionately and reaffirmed that rescuing our son would not help him recover.

Not too long after, we learned that Jonny had been walking in the snow to look for work and found a job at a restaurant. I felt grateful that at least he could get some food there. Then a few weeks later came another disturbing call.

"Mom, I've scraped together all but thirty-five dollars of the rent," our son said. "The apartment manager is here, and he's going to kick me out."

My heart was breaking, and my stomach was churning. How could I let my child be turned out onto the snow-covered streets? I saw no other choice. I reacted to his pain as well as mine. I wired him the money. Later, I sought counsel from my higher self.

> *h.s. You feel constricted as if you are wrapped in heavy chains from which you can't break loose. Don't fight. It's useless. All of your strength can never free you. Only God's strength can perform such a feat. You are so focused on the problem that you forget to pray, to call on your Deliverer. Whenever you feel this oppressive force overwhelming you, slap yourself awake with this thought, "I need help." Then let go of your son and the situation, and ask for help. Focus on the One who frees you. Focus on the end result, the peace and deliverance, and the breaking of the chains. Know this. Whenever you are in pain, help is available. Reach to the One who delivers you. Ask how to see the person and the situation in a different way, and light will pour into your soul, and you will see.*

The Wellness Community was temporarily without an administrative assistant. I saw an opportunity to focus on something besides my son, so I offered to fill in for several weeks until they could hire someone. The program director also asked if I would host a new class called "Dancing the Child Within." I welcomed this creative endeavor as another pathway to peace. But there was not enough response to fill the class, and it only lasted a couple of sessions. Still, I was struck by the synchronicity, which comforted me with the reassurance of some kind of grand design beyond my earthly knowing.

One of the center's staff psychologists was a dear, kind man. I spoke with him occasionally about Jonny. His gentle suggestions and wise observations comforted me. Then one day as I talked on the phone with my girlfriend, I heard myself singing this man's praises a little too loudly.

I asked myself, "Am I developing a crush on him, too?"

I resolved to keep my affection for this man in check, so I was keeping a careful watch on my self. But I was getting a little annoyed with my crazy sex chakra that seemed to be working overtime to get unblocked. I wondered if I had quit therapy too soon, before I worked through the transference with Dr. Tom.

I began reorganizing and cleaning out my bookshelves. It was not a quick process though because I couldn't resist getting reacquainted with portions of several books I'd read before. I love *A Path with Heart*, Jack Kornfeld's powerful guide to spiritual awakening. Passages in it reminded me how we all attempt to skip over our sorrows and wounds on our journey. The author says that we must connect with our body, our feelings, and our life just as it is now. There are no shortcuts.

One night as I watched a TV show about a woman who had been victimized as a child, I started to cry. Ted told me that I was stuck in the past. I reacted angrily. He said he was only telling me this out of love. I told him I didn't need that kind of love. My sad feelings were triggered easily these days. I wished I were not so sensitive, which meant, I suppose, that I wished I were not myself. When I wrote in my journal, there was a penetrating question.

> *h.s. What do you want to get over? Feeling? You have avoided feeling all of your feelings for too long. If you don't feel the sadness, you won't be able to feel the joy*

*either. As you open to all of life and its flow, you are
a complete person. You are a passionate person. Feel
and be.*

The term "spiritual bypass" came to mind. Author Jacquelyn Small and others described it as the temptation to use spiritual practices to avoid dealing with our childhood issues or earlier pain. I asked myself if I'd been guilty of this. Nearly a year earlier, Dolfi had first told me that I needed to make peace with my past. Why couldn't I just get this healing thing over with?

I had not seen Dr. Tom for several months, and yet, when I sometimes thought of him, those crazy lovesick feelings returned. As I looked within, I became more and more aware of a disturbing presence, a kind of sticky substance oozing up from the darkness. Then one day, I recognized it as shame. All along, I had thought that the love I'd felt for my therapist was my problem. Instead, perhaps the shame I had about those feelings may have been the real culprit!

I began to realize how often and deeply I condemned myself about this issue. I judged myself as foolish and immature. "What is wrong with you? You should be ashamed of yourself!" I had this attitude toward myself. I had just been hiding those exact words.

Years earlier, I had cried through nearly every page of John Bradshaw's book, *Healing the Shame That Binds You*. It had been such a relief to finally learn that there was a name for much of the pain I'd experienced and discounted throughout my life, codependency. Bradshaw says that toxic shame, the sense of failing and falling short as a human, is the basis of this addiction.

"If only someone would love me," it says. "But how could they? I'm not worthy of their love."

If I were ashamed of my feelings, I was ashamed of myself. I probably allowed that self-negation to play a part in my decision to stop the therapy. Maybe I had thought Dr. Tom was judging me, the same way I adjudicated myself. Even though my higher self kept giving me affirming, encouraging messages, I was still struggling with depression. The pain I had about my son nearly overwhelmed me at times. And then, I recently found my troubling tendency toward infatuation emerging when someone showed me a little kindness.

Did I need to get back in therapy? As soon as this thought arose, I judged myself as being self-indulgent to consider spending all that time and energy, not to mention money, on trying once again to get my act together. A couple of very close, wise friends had told me that they thought some further therapy would be a good idea. Why should I ignore their suggestions? I asked for help.

> *h.s. You must learn to love yourself. How can you love anyone or anything else unless you do? The time is now. I can help you. Books can help. You don't have to see, Tom, but it could help, he could help you very much. Do something for yourself. Take care of yourself. You deserve it. Don't be afraid. Have I failed you ever? Believe! Believe in your self and the love of God for you. Believe in the goodness of yourself and of life and others. Peace be with you.*

In spite of some reluctance, even fear, I made an appointment with Dr. Tom. The night before I was to see him, I had this dream.

> *My neighbor comes over and asks, "Have you finished your sin yet?" I know she is referring to a piece of needlework. I say, "No, I've just started, but I'm sure I'll like it once I get going." I ask her how to spell the word, S-I-N or S-Y-N?*

My real-life neighbor was someone who obviously lacked self-esteem. In the dream, she represented that same issue in myself. The needlework was my recovery path or inner work. "Sin" was the condition in which I saw myself as separate from God and judged myself as unworthy and guilty (the source of my shame). "Syn"

---

seemed to refer to working together with the therapist. Maybe I had just started. I was hopeful I would like the results, that is, I would achieve a greater peace of mind and heart that I'd been longing for.

As I prepared to go back to my shrink and my inner work, I made two more journal entries, a prayer and some second thoughts.

> *Dear God, Thank you for life, love, and blessings. Guide me to whatever road I am to take for my greatest healing. Bless Tom in his guiding me.*
>
> *Tues. p.m. I'm starting to second-guess myself. I wonder what Tom will think about my return. Will he think I'm making up an excuse to see him again? There I go, focusing on someone else, not myself! I thought I was learning about trusting myself spiritually. Yet, on a deep feeling level, I think I'm much more insecure. Think, think, think! Boy, do I want to avoid feeling!*

Chapter 16

*M*Y FRIEND PAULA HAD BEEN SEEING A COUNSELOR. ONE day in a phone conversation, she was talking about her therapy and mentioned a question that her therapist had suggested writing about: "What I wish my mommy had said?" This struck a chord in me, so I tried this exercise myself. It brought up a lot of deep feelings.

The date of my therapy appointment with Dr. Tom arrived. It was good to see this dear man again after nearly six months. But I also felt kind of dumb, like I had flunked out of Psychology I and had to repeat the course. I filled him in on all that had happened since I last saw him. I said I wanted to read something that expressed some of the unfinished issues I needed to address.

What I Wish My Mommy Had Said to Me

I love you very, very much. I'm so glad you're here. I'll always love you and protect you. You are such a special person to me. I want you to be and do everything that you want. I will teach you to listen to the deepest part of you and encourage you to follow the desires of your heart. If you're hurt, come to me, and I'll hold you close to my heart and comfort you. I will always have time for you. I will always listen to you. I will never try to mold you or force you to do something that demeans or demoralizes you. I will always respect you and teach you to respect

*yourself. I will never compare you to anyone else. You are
totally unique and perfect as you are. I will hold, soothe,
kiss, and comfort you when you are sad and laugh with
you when you are happy. I will always love you.*

While I was reading this to Dr. Tom, I began to cry a little. It was the first time this ever happened in his office. Before, I was always trying to be in control. At the end, he thanked me for reading it. I had been scared and reluctant about returning to therapy, but my inner wisdom was gently nudging me forward.

*h.s. You have opened a window. Breathe the refreshing
air. Don't allow it to close again. Treasure yourself
always. You are the greatest gift you have been given.
Affirm, affirm, affirm. Hug yourself, and dance with
yourself. Sing your own praises to yourself. The sun is
shining though the rain of your tears is falling. Look! A
rainbow! Life is good. Rest. Know. Love.*

Lucia Capaccione, PhD. , an art therapist and author of *The Power of Your Other Hand*, an art therapist, speaks about accessing the emotional and intuitive centers of the right hemisphere (visual/spatial) of the brain. The author suggests writing with the nondominant hand in order get in touch with the inner child. I tried this practice and found it quite amazing. In my notebook, I had regular written conversations between Big Kathleen (my right, dominant hand) and Little Kathy (left hand).

Big Kathleen: Dear Little Kathy, I wonder how your childhood was for you. I'd like you to tell me everything. You can trust me. I'll take care of you. I want to help you.

Little Kathy: Dear Big Kathleen, Well, I forget. Go find a picture of me. It might help us to remember. I'm feeling kind of chilly. Do you have a sweater?

At my next visit with my parents, I asked if they had some extra pictures of me as a child. I brought a small box of old snapshots home with me. As I started looking back more, I felt reluctant, as if I were about to clean out a cluttered old attic. When painful memories came up, it would have been easier to just repress or discount them. But they were not going away. I needed to sort things out and get rid of what was no longer serving me.

I am in grade school. My family has just finished dinner.
I pick up my dishes and start to carry them to the sink.
"Here, give me those," Mommy says. "I don't want you
breaking them. You know how clumsy you are."

On the way to a movie one night, Ted and I started talking about some topics I was looking at in my childhood.

He said, "Don't you see how angry you are at your mother? Have you told your therapist about this?"

I knew my husband had a difficult time dealing with anger. But I really wanted him to have some understanding of me. Later, at home, I get up the nerve to read him "What I Wish Mommy Had Said."

"No one is capable of that," he said, "but God."

"Of course I know that," I told him.

I knew intellectually that she did the best she could. But my little inner child hadn't really gotten it because she was still hurting. I wanted to help that hurting part of me. He didn't understand. We ended up in an argument. I prayed for guidance.

h.s. You have had mental pictures of the love of God for
you. This has been your wisdom's message for some time.
Yet mental pictures are not enough. You must feel this

certainty throughout your entire being. You must know it in your soul. The darkness must be enlightened. The grip of pain must be loosened. When you let go of the armor that has constricted and imprisoned you, then you will be free. The tentacles of despair do not loosen easily when they have been clutching at you for so very long. But you need not despair though you are tempted to believe that this pain will always be present. Your freedom is drawing nearer. Believe and it will be so. Don't push yourself out of your heart. Be tender and gentle with yourself. Embrace yourself.

The next morning, I had some quiet, tender moments with Ted, and he gave me a nice, long massage. We later went to a large party. He glided easily and laughingly through the crowd while I lingered at the bar, refilling my glass with wine.

I walk in the door from school and plop my books down on the kitchen table. "What did you get on the English test?" Mommy asks me. "Ninety-five," I say. "Oh," says Mommy. "What did Karen get?" Karen is my best friend at school. She is really smart and gets very good grades. Sometimes, her grades are higher than mine are. Karen tries very hard to please her daddy. I wonder if she's doing better with him than I am with Mommy.

It was nearly time to leave for my session with Dr. Tom. I recognized how tense I was feeling. My stomach was queasy, and my shoulders were tight. I felt vulnerable, like someone was going to rip off my clothes and put me on a platform in the middle of a town square where everyone would make fun of me. I wanted to cover myself and hide. I reminded myself to breathe deeply, relax, and get in touch with the moment.

After therapy, I felt more relaxed. I was getting better at accessing my feelings during a session. But it was still hard. I felt much freer at home to get in touch with and feel any deep feelings. During the session, there was a moment when I felt jarred. Dr. Tom offhandedly referred to his wife by her name. Before, she had been just a person in a picture on his desk. Now she was a real person with an actual name, not generic.

> *Dear Little Kathy, I love you. I'm so sorry that you couldn't be happy. I want to take care of you now. Back then, Daddy helped, but Mommy was sad and angry, and you didn't know why. You did your best. You learned to tune out, to escape inside where it was dark and quiet. But you missed so much of your little life. I want you to come back now. I want to teach you and me how to stay in our life, how to live completely, instead of always wanting to escape. I love you. Let me hold you very close. Mommy just could not do it. I'm sorry for you, her, and me.*

One dark, gloomy day, I made a series of telephone calls to handle a mistaken billing. I was frustrated. As the matter proceeded, I become furious. I went to my room, closed the door, and noticed what was happening in my body. My belly was hard, and my hands were clenched. I started crying. I felt afraid that I wouldn't be able to do all this work. I wrote about my anger, frustration, and fear, but I still felt stuck. So, I put down the book, picked up a plastic baseball bat, and started hitting some pillows. Finally, exhausted, I fell onto my bed.

> *I was very pregnant with our third child, Andrew. Ted and I were invited to a formal occasion. I tell my mother on the phone that I'm having a hard time finding something to wear. "Well, you asked for it", she snaps. After the call, I lie on the bed, sobbing. I feel stupid for having told her. I know how she feels about pregnancy and babies.*

Stephen Levine is one of my favorite authors. He and his wife Ondrea have done extensive work with the dying. In their book, *Healing into Life and Death,* he speaks of their healing work with abused women. He refers to the womb as a second heart, a place where much unhealed grief and pain can be stored. His beautiful "Opening the Heart of the Womb" meditation in this book and on tape helped me after I first uncovered the repressed rape. I wanted to go deeper into forgiving myself for any lingering feelings of guilt. I also realized how much I had rejected my female self. I had a hysterectomy a few years earlier. But I still felt led to address a letter to that unloved part of me that I had often seen physically and metaphorically as a source of suffering.

Dear soft, sweet, tender source of life, Please forgive me for my hatred, resentment, and inability to be open to the divine transmission of life. I was so sad and wounded. I could not see or feel. I felt so empty, so dead. May I now be opened to the possibility of life as I open to love, to sweet, tender care and forgiveness for myself. Please, God, melt the ice, the solid, cold rock that lies within me unmoving and unfeeling. Fill me with tenderness, love, and mercy for my inner child, as only I, her mother, can love her. Fill me with tender, gentle, sweet love for my own children, who have suffered by having started their lives in a cold and barren environment. May I forgive myself. I gave what I had to give then. May they learn to parent themselves with mercy. Open my heart to the child in us all, as I love my beautiful, innocent child in me so totally and completely with forgiveness. Amen.

Chapter 17

ONE WEEKEND, TED WAS SO BUSY WITH GOLF, FISHING, and yardwork that he barely seemed to notice me. I found myself feeling upset.

> **Little Kathy:** Why does he always leave me? I feel so lonely. Doesn't he know how bad I feel? You left me, too, Big K. I'm not too sure that you can take care of me either.

> **Big Kathleen:** I'm sorry. You're right. I'm so new at this job of taking care of you. I've been good at taking care of other people, but you're part of me. What do you need from me?

> **Little Kathy:** Will you pleaz spend some time with me? Don't be rushing off to get things done. That's what Mommy did. She wuz always cleaning, working, busy. When you do spend time with me, you feel gilty that you should be doing other things. Can't you just relax and love me?

> **Big Kathleen:** I'm sorry I have ignored you for so long. I'm sorry you feel so alone. I want to blame someone: Mommy, God, the Church, or Ted. But

most of all, I blame me. I was just always trying to be what everybody else wanted me to be. How could I hear your precious little voice? I'm sorry.

I realized that I had barely mentioned my father to Dr. Tom in the nearly year and a half since I'd been seeing him. I began looking at old pictures of my dad and thinking about him. Before long, I decided to write a letter to him in my journal.

Dear Daddy, Where were you when Mommy was yelling? Why didn't you stop her? I know you loved her. Didn't you love me, too? I remember you telling us stories and showing us cartoons. I remember your wonderful sense of humor and your kindness. But where were you when Mommy was so angry at us kids? Why didn't you tell her to stop? You must have had a hard childhood, Daddy. Can't you understand then how I felt? I guess you must have done the best you could. And if you were less funny and kind and nurturing, I don't know how we kids would have survived. But where were you when she was so angry? I love you, Daddy, and I thank you for all the sacrifices you made. Thank you for some happy memories when I was little. I will always feel sad when I hear Mommy put you down and treat you with disrespect. But I will also wonder, 'Where were you when Mommy was yelling?'

After I read "Dear Daddy" to Dr. Tom, he said something like, "So you didn't even realize you were angry with your father."
"Angry?" I questioned.
That was a surprise. I thought I was just mostly sad.

Our older son called to wish his dad a happy birthday. So often when I picked up the phone, I was afraid it was another crisis. I heard his voice that day, and my heart sank into my stomach. It was a short conversation: Was he all right? (What does *all right* mean?) My heart was pounding. I asked questions and then wondered why. I didn't really want to hear the answers.

> *h.s. Breathe slowly and deeply. Where you are going is nowhere. Come back to your self. Come back to God. You and all are cared for and divinely protected. Be still. Listen. Breathe. You know where to go, and there is nothing to do but trust. Put all your faith and trust in me and the me in your soul.*

I reread a section of *Creating Love*, which spoke of resentment toward our parents. As long as we hold on to it, the author, John Bradshaw, said we never grow up. It is a way of keeping us attached to them. Both idealization and resentment keep us bonded to our survival figures. I realized that my mother was neither a saint nor a sinner. She was just a person like me with good qualities and deficiencies alike.

John Bradshaw had many healing exercises in his books. In one, he suggests imagining your parent in the hospital, dying. Then you receive a phone call that the parent wants to say she is sorry. In another scenario, you can create a conversation between your child within and your parent's inner child.

I decided to try that second one. In my mind, I became very young, and I met my mother as a child at the small, second-story flat where we lived as children. This was an interesting experiment in which I realized that my mother as a child experienced much of the same insecurity and pain as I did.

One day, I slept very late, moving slowly most of the morning. I tried to meditate, but all the things on my to-do list gathered forces to distract me. There was a battle between my intention to be still, to focus on my breathing, and my intense desire to get moving. A body scan revealed a lump in my throat and pain in my side. Tears began.

> *Dear Mommy, Why did you have to be right all the time? Why were you so harsh, so bossy, and so mean? Couldn't you have been soft, tender, sweet, and kind like mommies should be? I didn't deserve such a mean mommy. I've hated having to carry all this pain around. What were you like under all the anger and harshness? Was there any softness or vulnerability? What were you afraid of: your father, God, life, or the Church? I don't know who you are. I just wish you had been someone else. You look so pretty in that picture with Daddy and me. Were you happy then? When did it all go? I'm so sorry, Little Mommy, that you hurt, too, just like I did. But why didn't you do something about it?*

Tears were coming so easily. But I couldn't grasp why. I recalled Stephen Levine writing in his book, *Meetings at the Edge* that "Letting go of our pain is the hardest work we will ever do and the most fruitful."

> *Dear Higher Power, Help me to break through my armor and clear out the garbage. Help me to trust the "don't know." Help me to let all be just as it is. May I be merciful to my self. May I invite love and acceptance into my self. May I treat my self as my only child. May I be cleansed of the pain of being a child. May I have the grace to let go of the pain. I have held it for so long.*

Chapter 18

OUR DAUGHTER AND SEAN WERE ENGAGED! WE WERE SO happy for them. They kept changing their minds about where the wedding would be. I encouraged them to decide soon because I'd heard that planning a wedding could take a long time.

That exercise from John Bradshaw's book about encountering my dying parent in the hospital was floating through my mind, but I kept putting it off.

> *h.s. Be patient with yourself. Don't rush or force yourself. Your grieving needs time. Yes, it hurts. That's all right. You can handle it. You can deal with yourself in a kind, gentle, loving way, the way you wanted your mother to do. Don't rush yourself. Time is a relative concept. Time is unimportant. Forgiveness is. Forgive yourself. You blame yourself for too much. You are innocent. Your mother is, too, but wait for the sun to rise by itself in due time. You need not turn on artificial light to see. Treat yourself with kindness. Get to know your unique beauty, the perfect irreplaceable person that you are. Be kind and gentle with your mother, too. Pray for patience, understanding, and acceptance of her. You know in your head she is doing what she can do, but your heart will grow into acceptance if you love and accept yourself without reservation. You are loved. You can love yourself. All is well.*

I had recently started reading *The Artist's Way*. I was excited about this wonderful book. I knew I was a very creative person. The author, Julie Cameron, kept telling me that I needed to nourish and nurture that part of me. She helped me to realize how I've put myself last on my priority list for so long, thinking mostly of others and their needs. I yearned to change that and asked for help.

> *h.s. Dear one, you are so precious, an essential part of the universe. Keep on working on forgiveness, especially of yourself, and you are home. Come home to your self. Nourish your self. Ask yourself often through the day: "Am I loving my self?" Take a walk. Be in touch with nature. Be in touch with yourself. All is well.*

Then it happened one day. I got that inner call that John Bradshaw had suggested in his book. My mother was dying in the hospital, and she wanted to tell me she was sorry. I decided to respond. And I also brought Little Kathy, my inner child, along with me.

> **Big Kathleen:** *Mommy is dying, little Kathy. We're going to go see her. She's sorry.*

> **Little Kathy:** *I want to believe her. Maybe she's lying. Pleaz. hold me. My tummy hurts.*

> **Big Kathleen:** *I am holding Little Kathy in my arms as I go into the hospital room. I question myself, "Can I do this? What does it all mean? I still feel angry. Why did it take so long?"*

> *Then I looked at my poor, little, old, withered Mommy. Her armor had softened. She had no more defenses. Little Kathy held me tighter. She was afraid. I patted her reassuringly. "This will help us," I said. I sat down*

on the bed and drew close to Mommy. She looked awful. She was barely breathing. I was crying. I questioned internally, "Why? What does it all mean? Please, God, help me."

Mommy said, "I'm so sorry. I love you. Will you forgive me for hurting you? I was in so much pain. I didn't want to hurt you."

"Yes, yes. I forgive you, I said. I know you didn't mean it. You did hurt me very much. But that's over. We can heal now. We can put it behind us. We both allowed it to be like that just so we could learn what loving and forgiving means. It's all just been for our healing, Mommy."

I took Mommy's and Little Kathy's hands and joined them. And I hugged them both, too. "We love you, Mommy. You can rest now. We can all let go. We don't have to resent you anymore 'cause that's in the past. And we're here now. And we can trust that everything that went before was meaningful in the light of our present love and forgiveness. May we all be healed. May we all be free. May we all be at peace. Amen."

I went through a lot of tissues that day. A couple of days later, I found the forgiveness process with my mother continuing at a church funeral service.

The priest sprinkles holy water and then swings the incense container over her casket. He says some prayers, and everyone answers, "Amen."

I think of Mommy in the closed casket, at peace at last, and I cry. I'm sorry for all her pain and mine. I pray we have all learned what we needed to experience for our ultimate healing. I'm grateful I could forgive her and myself. I breathe deeply and let her go.

I took some old family pictures to my next therapy session and I read my forgiveness meditation to Dr. Tom.

"Have you thought of actually telling your mother you had forgiven her?

I pondered that a bit and replied, "No."

"I just wanted you to be prepared if you decide to tell her that it may not turn out as peacefully as in your vision."

"I know. What really matters," I replied, "is what has taken place in my heart. I think I will keep that experience and treasure it there."

Rebecca's wedding was planned to be in St. Louis. We found a place for the ceremony, but we needed someone to perform it. A friend from my Wednesday morning group knew a minister, Reverend Joan. I called her, and we had a lengthy chat. She was a few years younger than I, and her spiritual journey had also led her out of traditional religion. Every Wednesday evening, a group met in her home to pray, share, and study. Ted and I went to meet Reverend Joan there. When Becca and Sean next came to town, they put their stamp of approval on her.

During a therapy session, Dr. Tom referred to Dolfi as "she," and I was taken aback. It caused me to reflect. I'd always thought of Dolfi as male.

"Why was that?" I wondered.

I started to play around with making my dolphin spirit guide female, but it just didn't work. I knew both men and women had some hormones and characteristics of the opposite sex. So, maybe Dolfi was a symbol of the male part of me. That was an interesting idea. He did seem strong, assertive, and sure of himself. Those were qualities I could use some work on. Come to think of it, that's what I had been working on.

The wedding took up residence in a large area of my mind. One day, I wondered what some of our very conservative friends and relatives would think about a female minister officiating at Rebecca's wedding. I asked Ted how he would feel about God if "She" had always been adored, written about, prayed to, and thought of as a woman. My husband just stared blankly at me. I suppose the subject was beyond his imaginings. Sometimes, I directed our dinner table prayers to "Father/Mother God," which Drew found a good opportunity for some lighthearted jabs at his mom. He laughingly conceded that the devil may perhaps be female, but he was quite certain that God was male. (This from an avowed atheist!)

In an attempt to undo years of brainwashing, for a while I focused on what I saw as my Creator's "feminine" qualities. I thought of "Her" as tender, nurturing, warm, sensitive, and gentle. But I really preferred the term "Spirit." It brought me closer to my goal of seeing God as I believe He or She is, neither sex exclusively, but embodying "All That Is."

My friend Jan called from Phoenix. She was feeling down. I listened for a while and then told her how good she was. I told her what Buddha said, "You could search the whole world over and not find anyone more worthy of love than your self." I repeated what I'd heard on one of the Stephen Levine tapes, "Treat Yourself Like Your Only Child." She perked up and seemed to feel better before we hung up. Afterward, I smiled as I realized I was doing that "teaching and healing" thing that Dolfi told me to a while back.

Chapter 19

WE RECEIVED ANOTHER DISTURBING PHONE CALL from Jonny. He said a good friend told him he needed to stop using drugs and he was going to. We had suspected his drug use for some time, but it was finally out in the open. Ted told him he needed to attend twelve-step meetings and get a sponsor.

"Maybe," he said.

Once again, he refused our offer to pay for therapy. I felt devastated.

> *h.s. Pain is a terrible distraction to truth. But it is also an arrow and points the way to truth. The pain is still pointing the way. But don't be tempted to focus on the arrow. Focus on your destination: truth, peace, and wholeness. In focusing on the pain of your son, you have misplaced your attention. He is not the problem. It's how you see him. You have looked for salvation and truth outside your self because you felt so empty inside. Release. Cut the cord that binds you to him.*

The holidays were approaching. It was not my favorite time of year. I had many early memories of what I describe as craziness around these days, weeks, and months. And I tended to see the spirit of Christmas as mostly materialistic. I decided to focus instead on the trip we had planned for Phoenix early in January.

I called my sister one day. In the course of the conversation, she said an engagement party was being held for my niece, Kathryn, by her future mother-in-law. She mentioned several people who would be there and then added quickly, "But I was sure you and Ted wouldn't want to come."

I was stunned! "What?" I thought I had misheard her.

"Well, so-and-so are coming, but I knew you two wouldn't want to."

My heart sank. "That's not true."

There was silence. I felt sick to my stomach and tried to cover up my embarrassment at the perceived rejection.

"Well, we will probably be in Phoenix around that time anyway." This was only partially true because our tickets were open-ended. I found some excuse to quickly end the call.

At my next appointment with Dr. Tom, I told him about the phone call.

"I couldn't believe what she said."

"Well, maybe you misunderstood her. Would you consider calling her again?"

"Are you serious?" I asked him.

"Sure," he replied. "What have you got to lose?"

I felt fearful about his suggestion, but I decided to try it.

"Pam," I said, nervously," I just wanted to make sure about what you said at our last phone call. I felt "disinvited" to Kathryn's party and it hurt me."

"Well, I'm sorry," she replied, curtly, but I've been hurt, too." And then she hung up!

I felt shaken, as if I'd stepped out into the street and been nearly hit by a vehicle. I took a couple of deep breaths and cleared my thoughts. My sister was obviously still carrying hurts from many years. I was certain my grandmother's favoritism of me must have been difficult for her. It must have also been frustrating for Pam to have an older sister who seemed so perfect. Of course, she could not see the pain I was carrying from trying to live up to my family's expectations of me. Yes, we'd both been hurt. But I wanted to have a relationship with her. Over the years, I'd tried so hard to get her to like me, walking on eggshells, fearful of saying or doing anything that might make her feel worse. But it didn't seem to help.

I took out some old snapshots of us kids. On most of them, I was standing like a little mommy with my arms around my slightly younger siblings. I wanted to tell Pam how sad I felt, but I was afraid she would just hang up again on me. I picked out an especially appealing picture and sent it to her with a note that said simply, "The way we were." I hoped she might remember.

Our trip to Phoenix was fun. But I still felt upset about things back home. I told a friend about my problems with my sister. She said that she and her younger sister went to a shrink together. They found it helpful in working out some of their relationship difficulties. I wondered if I could get Pam to go to a counselor with me.

When I returned, I called my parents and asked them how my niece's party was. They said it was very nice and about seventy-five people were there. I felt like I'd been slapped in the face.

I started crying. "She didn't even invite me," I sputtered.

"You're lying!" my mother snapped. "Pam said she invited you. What do you care anyway? You were never interested in the family."

I felt small and powerless, like a child. As my mother's accusations continued, I foolishly got locked into trying to defend myself. Then I felt guilty. My parents were very old after all. I told my mother I didn't mean to upset her and I loved them both. But I felt sad.

One cold, dreary winter day, I was feeling discouraged about my family of origin. Morever, the family I'd created wasn't doing so hot either. Andrew was doing poorly in school. Ted and I were distant as I was often spinning my emotional wheels about our sons, my parents and sister. I knew life was good and beautiful, but it was hard to see it that day.

h.s. Holidays come and go, but you go on. Focus only on the love. Seize on any tiny spark of the eternal fire, and watch it and love it as it flickers, burns, and then glows with great intensity. Love your self, your life, and everyone therein. It is a valid, worthy, good life, no better or worse than any other but part of the entire plan. Do not resist any facet of your story. It is all essential. Rejoice. You are participating in the divine mystery. You need not understand. Indeed, you cannot. You need to experience, participate, embrace, and love. That is all. Do not try to experience the entirety at once. That's what days, hours, and seconds are for. All is as it is to be. You are where you are to be. Only love and leave the details to me.

I decided to wrap up my second round of therapy with Dr. Tom. Plans for the upcoming wedding were keeping me busy and seemed like therapy enough. I was having fun with this creative project. But as I thought of not seeing my counselor anymore, I felt sad. I had a lingering attachment to him and still felt a little embarrassed about it. I wanted those feelings to be gone.

h.s. Just be with the feelings. Just hold them in your heart as you would hold your treasured infant. Hold them; love them. Don't try to figure them out or get rid of them. Don't be sorry that you love. When you experience a loss on the physical level, know that you are not a body. I know it feels like you are. It hurts. I know. Just let the tears come. It's all right. I love you. There were so many others in your life from whom you wanted love, and you didn't feel it coming to you. But that's all right. They just were unable to give you that love, to give you what you thought you needed. But that didn't mean you were unworthy or unloved.

Nearly two years had passed since Dolfi came into my life. Yes, my dolphin friend was still around, somewhat in the background. Now and then, I'd call on him. I'd made some more emotional progress this year. And I'd sometimes fallen backward. This life thing was an amazing, mysterious journey. I was grateful for so many blessings, including my inner voice that kept me on the path when I was tempted to stray. I prayed to be more open in listening to the important truths it conveyed.

> *h.s. Do not look where you've been. Look only where you are. There is light enough in the moment for you to see. Touch yourself tenderly with mercy. You are learning. But the learning continues. Gratitude for the moment is very important. You do not want to stay in the role of victim, not the real you, but the sad, lonely, desperate, illusory you. You are so comfortable with that stance that you are struggling with throwing off that cover of darkness. That's all right. You do not have to be perfect now. You do not have to understand it all now. Don't put impossible demands on yourself. Relax. Lighten up. Let the world evolve. Let yourself learn gradually in due time. Listen. Be still. Feel. Know. Love. Let go.*

As the wedding drew nearer, things got especially hectic. But I had decided from the start that I would not let the details drive me crazy. My regular quiet time, prayer, meditation, and messages from my inner wisdom helped me walk peacefully amidst the occasional chaos.

The guest list was a challenge. We had to limit numbers to keep costs down. Ted and I discussed our feelings about inviting my sister and her family to the bridal shower and wedding. I still felt hurt but also wanted to keep the peace, such as it was. A bridal shower for Becca was held at my house. It was a lovely event. Though members of my family were invited, none attended.

I had spent so much of this year still focusing on others: my family of origin, my children, and my husband. I prayed to find my way to myself more clearly in the year ahead.

Chapter 20

I MANAGED TO KEEP MY COOL ABOUT THE WEDDING plans until the very last week. After the final fitting, Becca was in tears. She thought her dress was too short. We spent the greater part of two days looking for very flat shoes. I was about to suggest that she go barefoot.

At last, the day arrived. All the details fell in place, and all our hard work was rewarded. The wedding and reception were glorious. The event went much too quickly, but when it was over, I felt relieved, proud, and happy. It was a perfect evening. Or so I thought.

About a week later, on the way to a movie, I told my friend Meg that I was thinking of having a bridal shower for my sister's daughter. She looked troubled but said nothing.

As I talked further about my plans, she broke her silence. "Kathy, please stay away from your sister."

"What do you mean?" I asked.

"Did you get an invitation to Carol Grant's wedding anniversary?"

"What?" I asked. "Don't try to change the subject. Just tell me what you know about my sister."

"We were talking and I kept telling her how pretty and slim you looked and what a great job you did planning the wedding," she answered. "And every time I said something nice about you, she'd shoot right back with a criticism."

"Are you kidding me?"

"Why would I lie to you? "I was shocked," Meg said. "I probably should have walked away. I just wanted to defend you, Kath."

My eyes got teary.

My friend hugged me. "I don't want to see you experience any more pain from your family."

I was thrown into a storm of feelings, which tossed me around for days and weeks. I cried and prayed for guidance.

> *h.s. Go ahead and let the tears flow. Let the pain out. You can let all the pain go. You are so good and beautiful. I love you. The One who brought you into existence—your own heavenly Mother—loves you with a deep, powerful, never-changing, everlasting love. Go ahead and drink it in. Let every pore and cell in your body breathe in the love. Breathe in the deep, powerful, supportive, enlightening, uplifting, nourishing love that fills and surrounds you. How can you doubt or fear when the air you breathe, the stuff that gives you life, the essence of who you are, is love! You are love. Everyone is your sister and brother. You are not lacking family. Your whole life and whole world is filled with family. Some just don't know that. Tell them that. And if they don't listen or don't believe you, tell them once again. Yet they must decide to believe in their own hearts. And if, after the third time you tell them that God is their mother and you are their sister, then go. Move on to the next sister or brother. Not everyone will hear you. Each will decide to listen and believe when he or she is ready. The divine plan is perfect. You need not worry or control. Only believe. Only trust. Speak. Wait briefly. Then move on. Don't look back. Move on. Why be angry? Why be hurt? Others have reached out to you. You reach out to others. And so it goes. Be still. Be happy.*

Reverend Joan and I had become friendly during the wedding preparations. I told her of my dilemma. I wanted to be a loving, forgiving, spiritual person. I was also trying to love myself more. In order to be accepted by others, I sometimes allowed their disrespect and mistreatment. I had been nearly unaware that I had a choice. As I began to recognize I did have choices, I was still unsure how to implement them. I was grateful for Joan's loving suggestions that I first and foremost take care of myself.

An invitation to my niece's wedding shower arrived. Since Rebecca's wedding, I had not spoken with my sister. But, in an attempt to heal our relationship, I had written and rewritten numerous letters to her, trying to express my distress and sadness. Each letter was torn up, as I feared she would find fault, misunderstand, and criticize whatever I said. I cared for my niece, and I did not want to disrespect her. I wanted to honor myself as well. I asked for help.

h.s. Where to go? What to do? What to say? The questions keep you tied in knots. You want to do the right thing. That's what you've always wanted. There is no right thing. There are many right things, many good places, and many kind words. Let go of the questions. Rest secure in knowing that you will be guided as you let go. Yes, it's scary. You have hung on to the old, rotten pieces of floating garbage as you felt like your life was a struggle to stay afloat in the shark-infested waters. But you thought you were alone there. Your Mother God has always been there with you. Get into the boat of salvation, for it is there with your Holy Partner that you are safe. It is there you will and do know that you can rest secure. Yes, you must occasionally work at keeping the boat out of dangerous places, but you are not alone. And at those times when you are drifting safely, rest, relax, and trust, knowing that, if danger arises, you have all the resources to be, do, and say whatever you need.

After much prayer and some conversations with my inner child, I sent my regrets with a gift to my niece's shower and later her wedding.

I was still working at the Wellness Community. My volunteer position had evolved into a part-time job. The computer data entry work was not thrilling, but I liked being there. I thought of the people, the atmosphere, the good work being done, and the inspiration I received from the cancer patients and volunteers.

My journal remained a valuable tool in helping to clarify where I'd been and what I was learning. Once the wedding was over, I had more time, so I began transferring my notebook pages to the computer. As I did, I found new insights about myself. And I started to have a notion that someday I might put all my experiences together into manuscript form.

For so long, it was difficult for me to appreciate my unique talents or explore my own desires. Some years earlier, when a counselor had asked me what I wanted, I was speechless. I had seldom gotten in touch with what I wanted. For most of my life, I was taught to defer to what others—parents, husband, children, church, and community—wanted from me.

I have always enjoyed writing. But whenever I thought of seriously pursuing that calling, I felt afraid of failure and unworthy of success. I kept my light hidden. But I wrote in journals, dabbled at poetry, took a couple of writing courses, penned some short stories, and wrote volumes of letters to faraway friends. At one point, I began hearing unfamiliar melodies flowing through my mind. I somehow got the music notes down on paper. Lyrics came, too. I was then led to a musician/writer partner, and with the help of a vocalist friend, we spent the next couple of years composing and recording. None of our pieces were published, but it was a fun, creative experience for all of us. I learned a lot, and I have a large box of sheet music and tapes that we produced.

My inspirational messages were continuing, even increasing, as I learned to trust in myself and this process. In addition to my Dolfi adventures, I began compiling my messages only into a separate volume. When I worked and played on the computer, the time flew, and my heart sang.

> *h.s. Pour yourself into the words. Play and dance with them. Let go of trying to make them work. You need not do this. Let go of the need to control, and the words will sing. Force them, and they are mute. Flow into the words, the sentences, and the ideas just as you are doing now. You do not know what's coming next, like the play of life. Moment by moment the situations, the drama, and the meaning come into view. Enjoy.*

A wise therapist once asked me an important question, "When do you feel most like yourself?"

I thought a while and then replied, "When I am creating stories, poems, and songs."

It was a tiny bud of truth I uncovered then. That truth was blossoming into a lovely flower. I was learning to affirm such wisdom about my gifts and talents in order to counteract the part of me that was used to staying stuck in the role of a victim.

> *I am a cocreator! I create lovingly with God. I allow divine inspiration to flow through me. I am happy when I create. I nurture myself with love as I write. I am a cocreator with God! My creativity gives me power and peace.*

Despite the joy I had found by expressing myself creatively, I was still struggling to reconcile my place in my family of origin and my own family. I knew forgiveness was a worthy goal. I understood spiritually that all of us are one.

So why couldn't we live that way? I wondered. *Why couldn't my sister forgive me? And why couldn't I just let go of my hurt feelings, the sadness I felt about my failure to have a loving relationship with everyone in my world?*

I sometimes told myself I should be farther along spiritually, I should just be able to forgive, and I should be beyond these petty hurts and sad feelings. And yet most of my very wise teachers told me not to "should" on myself. I turned for support from my spiritual books. *A Course in Miracles* said to "beware of the temptation to see yourself unfairly treated." I recognized the wisdom of these words, but I could not deny the truth of what I was feeling either. Must I?

I looked to my fellow spiritual travelers. Some held me close physically and prayerfully, and I was comforted. Others quoted the same teachings, which I was allowing to convict me. For a while, I put away the sacred writings. For a time, I withdrew from a couple of my groups.

In the darkness, I had to find my own light, the truth of my own experience. While I felt weak, I had to find my inner strength. I knew my highest truth and strength were those of God, my higher power. But sometimes they lay hidden very deep within.

Chapter 21

ONATHAN GOT A DUI. IT HAD HAPPENED A WHILE AGO, but Ted didn't tell me when he heard about it, thinking it would get me too upset. I felt angry at our son and my husband. Then I realized the anger was just covering up my feelings of sadness and powerlessness I didn't want to feel. I was fearful, too. I was afraid that these sad scenarios would just keep repeating over and over.

> *h.s. Go to your Source. Trust that all is in divine hands. You are not holding the world. It is in the hands of God. Send your son love. Bless him, and thank him for his presence in your life, the great lessons you are learning and the opportunity, and this situation. This person provides for you to learn what you must learn. Remember, you are deserving of great and enormous respect. Love and hold yourself tenderly, and sing gentle lullabies to you, God's own precious child. In the eyes of God, your son is whole and holy and healed and healing. Be still. Go within, the only place to go. The answers to all your questions are there. Love. Be still. Trust. Know. Heal.*

Once again, the issue of our struggling son pulled Ted and me far apart from one other. When I was upset, Ted wanted to fix me or became very worried about me. We were having a challenging time. We decided to plan a vacation together with no one else along. We had not done that in a long time. Meanwhile, I kept working on relationship issues with my son (like guilt and forgiveness) and regularly wrote him letters (unmailed) in my journal.

> Dear Jonathan, I love you very much. I am sorry for anything I have ever done to hurt you. I never did so intentionally, but I am not always in touch with the deepest parts of myself. I ask your forgiveness. Please excuse my imperfection. I wanted to be a perfect mother. But I wasn't. Nobody is a perfect anything. Still, you deserve the best. And God is the only one who can give you that. I am grateful for the divine presence that is always with us, the one who can and does lead us to forgiveness and to healing. I pray that you can forgive me as I pray to forgive you. May our hearts be free of unforgiveness. May we be at peace.
>
> *h.s. Isn't it beautiful and good? You are learning. Your burdens don't have to stay with you. They can be lifted. They can be healed. Bless yourself, and thank yourself for getting unstuck. Thank your self for seeking and accepting healing. You deserve healing. I am here in your breath, in your heartbeat. Never forget. I am with your children. They are not alone. Nor are you. Life is good. All is well.*

My mother's throat had been very sore. She went to the hospital for tests. I waited to hear the results and wondered why it was taking so long. Finally, I called her. She answered and said she'd been home a while but didn't feel like talking. I asked to speak with my father.

"Why didn't you call me?" I asked impatiently.

He seemed embarrassed and began listing excuses for their lapse: a long wait at the hospital, Mom feeling so bad, and so forth.

I interrupted. "What's wrong with her?"

"She has throat cancer," he replied.

I began to cry.

"I'm sorry we didn't call," he said.

My mother's therapy required radiation twice a day for six weeks. I was concerned how they would manage. I decided, for my parents' sake, to call my sister.

"Pam," I asked her, "Could we put aside our differences to work out a plan for helping Mom and Dad?"

"What differences are you talking about? You're so weird, Kathy. Don't worry about Mom and Dad. I've got everything taken care of." Then she made some reference to my niece's wedding.

"Yes, Mom said it was very nice. I wasn't too enthused about attending her wedding after I heard about the remarks you made to Meg at Becca's wedding.

"Well, I'm sure that your so-called friend was totally truthful," she snarled, and launched into a scathing criticism of Meg.

"I have no reason to doubt Meg's sincerity, Pam, " I responded. And then I hung up.

> *h.s. You feel hurt. Your sister feels hurt. What does that mean? Neither of you is seeing clearly. There is a light beyond and within, but the fog of past illusions covers the landscape. You let yourself be pulled into the fog, and you got lost. Ego is seductive. Trust that truth is revealed with each step you take. Put aside for now the temptation to withdraw and to explain. Lift your sister and all in prayer. Wish no harm to anyone. Above all, seek no harm to your self. Protect your self. Hold her to your heart and know that love surrounds and comforts you always. Love is here and there for everyone. Wish no harm. Only bless yourself and all.*
>
> *What to learn? Though we are all one, we do not act as such. We see with many eyes when we look at*

> *the drama. But one vision sees Spirit. The view is clear and perfect. There is no distortion. Someday, we will see what we already are in truth. You can love without inviting disrespect. It takes balance, a careful walk on the tightrope of relationship. It takes much prayer, patience, and love. Be at peace. Let go. Let life reveal itself to you.*

I got word that my late uncle's wife was on life support. I went to the hospital to spend a little time with her and her family. Soon thereafter, she died. After my uncle had died four years earlier, my family of origin decided they wanted no further contact with his wife. When they found out that I still spoke with her occasionally, several family members expressed bitterness about my so-called betrayal. It was hard for me to receive such rejection. I felt grateful that I could bring a little comfort to our aunt and her family. The funeral, of course, brought up many painful issues of alienation and discord.

A dark cloud of depression was blocking my vision. My spirits were low, and it was hard to lift them. I wanted a higher perspective. I decided to go see Dr. Tom again to help me sort out some of these foggy issues. Before going, my inner wisdom gave me encouragement.

> *h.s. Holy are you. Say it. I am holy. I am good. I am worthy. I am deserving. I am pure. I am Spirit. I am free. That's right. Get up off the ground. Feel yourself lifting oh so slightly. I am innocent. (Lift your wings.) I am able: able to rise above, able to leave the past behind, and able to focus on the wind beneath my wings that lifts me ever so gradually up. I can do this. I am strong. I am powerful and stronger than all the forces around me: the gravity, the lethargy, the discouragement, and the tiredness. I can fill my lungs with cooling, fresh air. I can hold up my wings and I can see things from a distance, from above where the view is clearer. But I will not keep looking downward. I will focus ahead above, where I am*

and where I am going: to the sun, to the light, and to the
Love that oversees and holds it and us all together.

Ted and I had a nice trip to Santa Fe, but shortly after returning home, we began arguing again. We were so tired of the pain and unhappiness. We felt stuck. As scary and sad as the prospect was, we were considering the possibility of separation. Dr. Tom gave us the name of a marriage therapist. We felt reluctant to go through therapy, knowing it would probably entail a lot of work. We were a bit battle-scarred and weary. But we had a lot of time and energy already invested in this relationship. We decided it would probably be worth the effort.

Bill Warren, our new counselor, was definitely outside the mold. He was tall and slender. He wore jeans and boots and reminded me of Tim Robbins, the actor. During the sessions, he usually draped himself casually over a small couch, while Ted and I sat across from him on a larger sofa.

Unlike most therapists, Bill never took notes. But he had a keen memory. He always remembered things we had said and managed to make both of us feel at ease and understood. His office became a safe haven where Ted and I could open up, speak our truth, and really listen to one another. The gift of tears was a regular occurrence for each of us in this sacred space. And Bill's wonderful sense of humor eased the tension at times and gave us some good laughs.

It was difficult at first, as we started to take an honest, penetrating look at ourselves. We saw how much we clung to being right and blaming each other and how destructive that was. Bill guided us gently from our warring positions and lovingly urged us to put down our weapons. We were amazed to find that, behind the threatening swords dividing us, we were just a little girl and a little boy who were very afraid of not being loved.

We learned how we had been lugging around old, outworn baggage filled with misunderstanding, rejection, and resentment. As we let go of those burdens, we felt freer than we had in a very long time. Little by little, we got greater glimpses of the beauty that had always been inside and between us. Bill gave us communication tools to help us get us unstuck when we fell back into old cycles of blame and control. We resolved to make more time for each other and to treasure the amazing gift of our relationship.

The inner work I had been doing on myself was, I believe, a very important precursor to the success of our marriage counseling. Ted had told me often over the years that he loved me, but I had a hard time being able to receive that love, to actually believe that I was loveable. As I began to let in his love, I was surprised to find the depth of love and tenderness I felt toward my husband. We were finally giving birth to a more loving and intimate, satisfying relationship.

Bill told us that we were on the hero's journey. It made us proud of the hard work we were accomplishing through this process. We were grateful that we had chosen to push through the difficult pain we had been experiencing. And we were also thankful to have had the guidance of this loving, wise counselor.

Chapter 22

STEPHEN LEVINE IS ONE OF MY FAVORITE INSPIRATIONAL authors. He and his wife Ondrea were scheduled to give a weekend seminar at the Omega Institute in New York. When I had first read about it the previous spring, I wanted to sign up then. But Ted was not interested, so I began repressing my desire. I rationalized that it would cost too much anyway and was complicated to get there. I felt sad as I closed the Omega catalog and put it away.

An important lesson I'd been learning was how important it is for me to get in touch with what I really want and how to take care of myself. When I routinely deferred to others' wishes and thought only of *their* needs, I was not loving myself. The Levine workshop kept coming to my mind, and I started to recognize how much I really wanted to attend. So I asked Ted again. He said he had scheduled a business trip then. So I decided I'd go anyway. It felt good to acknowledge my own desires, to make my own decisions. Then shortly after I started making plans, Ted said he'd changed his mind and made arrangements to be free for the seminar. I called Omega and signed us up.

The topic of the Levine's weekend was his latest book, *A Year to Live*. On Friday night of the retreat, Stephen presented this hypothesis to the approximately five hundred attendees. Let us suppose, he said, that a doctor has just told each of us that we only have one year left to live. After receiving this news, we were to make two lists. The first would detail all the reasons why this diagnosis saddened us and why we wanted to keep on living. On the second list, we were to write the reasons why having only a year to live might be welcomed news.

On Saturday morning, the Levines began addressing the audience. Stephen spoke of the many terrible ways we treat ourselves. For example, he said, if we were seated next to ourselves at a restaurant and could overhear aloud the way we inwardly criticized ourselves, we would probably call the police.

"Have mercy on yourself," he said tenderly.

His words touched me deeply. Years of contempt, unkindness, and lack of forgiveness for myself filled my thoughts. Tears streamed down my cheeks. Stephen invited volunteers in the audience to approach any of several microphones around the auditorium, to share if we wished. With a surge of inspiration, I sprung from my seat and nervously took my place in line. Soon, it was my turn to speak.

I started by telling Stephen how much I had appreciated his work and what a gift he had been to me and to us. "I was very excited to be here when I arrived last night. But then, as I began to look around the room, I became discouraged. Everyone I saw seemed younger, more beautiful, better dressed, more educated, and more at ease with themselves than me."

"Ah," Stephen said, observing compassionately and nodding his head. "Comparing mind."

"My first list," I said, sputtering, responding to his questions, "presented the reasons why I didn't want to die. There were such earthly delights: a juicy fresh peach, my husband's or children's warm, tight hug, the magnificence of an Arizona sunset, the heart-touching words of a tender poem, the joy of sidesplitting laughter …" I trailed off. "And then," I said, sighing tearfully, "there is my second list. Why I would welcome the death verdict. I had only one entry," I whispered, barely able to speak. After a pause, I uttered, "Maybe now they'll appreciate me."

"Hmm," Stephen proclaimed with a twinkle in his eye and a sly smile. "Probably not!"

The crowd chuckled, and I smiled, too, as I wiped my eyes.

"I have spent far too long," I said, "focusing on others, trying anything I could think of to please, to get them to like me. I now know the greatest task before me during this supposed last year of my life. I have to stop waiting for others' approval. I simply must learn to appreciate and love myself."

There was a smattering of soft clapping as I remained standing, sniffling, in the aisle of the huge, white-tented auditorium.

Stephen directed some remarks to the audience. "Is this what it takes? Do we need to have a terminal disease in order to treat ourselves with mercy?"

He continued addressing the next audience member at the mike while I returned to my seat, weak from sadness, nervousness, and, finally, relief. I wasn't sure if what I said had made any sense.

At the end of this session, on our way out of the auditorium, a young woman approached me shyly. "Thank you," she said, "for what you shared. I think you spoke for a great many of us here, and you said it very well."

I smiled and thanked her. Wow! The universe had just given me a warm hug. I felt grateful for the confirmation of what my inner wisdom had been telling me for a long, long time.

> *h.s. You have turned a corner. The view is astounding. You cannot turn back. Leave your old world and your old self behind. You will not miss her, though a part of you is fearful that is so. Hold that fearful little child in your arms and tell her you love her. Tell her she is so beautiful and never ever alone. Tell her to take your hand and our hands and join you on this wonderful journey. The past is gone. It cannot touch her or hurt her. Only the love she has known, only the people crying for love she has known, and only the tender mercy she has felt from others and the universe are all that is left. All that remains is this precious instant, full of the possibility of forever through the mighty power of love, forgiveness,*

mercy, gentleness, and oneness. There is nothing to fear.
Have mercy.

Not long after we returned from the amazing Omega retreat, a phone call at 1:00 a.m. woke us. Our younger son, Drew, was at the police station. He had been arrested for possession of marijuana. When Ted brought him home, we could see Drew was frightened of losing his license and even his car. We had a long, open, honest talk with him. He told us this was an isolated incident and he was very foolish. We wanted to believe him.

I realized that this traumatic situation had provided us some leverage. I repeated an earlier concern I'd had about what I saw as depression in him. I said I thought he needed to see a counselor. He agreed to do so. Very soon, he began seeing a kind, wise therapist who was a positive influence on our young son. Something we had first labeled as "bad"—Drew's arrest—became an opportunity with hindsight. We were grateful for some favorable, healing results from this incident.

"Codependency" is about losing one's self in relationships. I had been aware of this problem of mine for nearly ten years. But I still danced around the issue in my denial and halfhearted attempts to heal from this tendency. Shortly after the Levine's workshop, I began falling back into old patterns of fear and worry about various issues, especially our sons. I looked for and found a CODA (Codependents Anonymous) meeting. After attending several different groups, I settled on one that I particularly liked.

There are a number of twelve-step meetings for various issues, but they are all similar in their emphasis on personal sharing and working the twelve steps adapted from Alcoholics Anonymous. Attending meetings with other honest, open people who are willing to look at our issues and work on our recovery "one day at a time" has proved to be an incredibly healing, life-changing experience. Once again, I got a message that the universe had been proclaiming to me with various voices for the last several years: I am not alone.

A long chapter of my story seemed to be wrapping up. My husband was offered a work opportunity in another state. We both felt positive about the offer. There were people and things we knew we'd miss about our home at the time, but we had learned from our previous move to Phoenix what an enriching experience moving can provide. We were happy that Drew chose to go with us.

I visited my parents and informed them and my siblings of our moving plans. I was learning to be grateful for these teachers of mine. I held them respectfully and prayerfully in my heart. My mother was recovering from throat cancer. Both she and my father were frail. I prayed that their remaining time on this earth would be peaceful and healing. I trusted that we would one day all heal from our pain and find complete forgiveness in our hearts for those whom we thought had hurt us, for all the illusions that kept us from healing. I was reminded of Stephen Levine's wise words: "There is no situation in which forgiveness is inappropriate, but it can take time."

Our older son, Jonathan, continued on his journey, changing jobs and cities numerous times. We heard from the twelve-step community that this was sometimes cynically called "the geographical cure." Through that same program, I began learning ever so gradually to lessen my concerns about his various paths, knowing they are his decisions and I can do little, if anything, about anyone else's healing but my own.

I said good-bye to my therapist once again. I was still fond of this kind, wise, funny guy who had helped me through some challenging and amazing times. But the lovesick feelings I once had for him had gradually evolved into a warm and tender gratitude for his support. I had somehow managed almost imperceptibly to "work through the transference" as I gained self-confidence and self-esteem.

I was learning to detach and let go of relationships and situations that were not nurturing. I began to know that I had choices when I was tempted to fall into codependency. I could instead choose to be a cocreator with God by expressing my own creativity. I was learning to appreciate myself. I was healing.

Those terrible panic attacks that had once plagued me were, thank God, a thing of the past. I had not had one since early in the Dolfi saga, nearly three years earlier. Those attacks were like the release of steam from a pressure cooker. All the energy from my blocked, repressed feelings had to escape somehow. As I learn to respect and allow my feelings and to express them in a nonharming manner, they no longer build up and have to escape in such a horrific way.

Depression and anxiety still challenge me at times, but they are lessening as I find healthy ways to deal with my issues. For us mystical Persephones who spend so much time in contemplative worlds though, this can be a weak spot at times of stress. I feel certain more healing lies ahead on my journey.

As I travel through the paths of life, I know there may be the occasional minefield that complicates my journey. But I am learning to take it one day and one step at a time. I can go gently, thoughtfully, meditatively, and prayerfully. I must know, nurture, and love my self. I regularly forget certain facets of all that I've learned. I need regular reminders.

Our move proved to be a definite God deal. The Internet helped me find other spiritually minded people in our new location. I quickly joined several small groups, including *A Course in Miracles* study as well as Al-Anon, a twelve-step fellowship for families and loved ones of alcoholics. I learned I could not take someone else's inventory, but I needed to learn how to take care of myself. Al-Anon is enormously helpful in learning about the disease of alcoholism/drug addiction, and I am learning skills to detach lovingly from our addicted loved ones.

Ted and I grew closer as our relationship became deeper. He and I joined hands again spiritually and found a church that reflected our newly similar values. It had been a while since I had been inside a church, but then, miracles do happen! And that's another story. It is time for me to complete this part of my tale.

Chapter 23
Reflections on My Mystical Journey

$\mathcal{W}$HEN I LOOK BACK AT THESE PRECEDING, TUMULTUOUS chapters of my life, I ask myself: What was the purpose of these mystical experiences? Then I remember the answer that came to me early on when I had questioned why such perplexing events were happening: I had to get your attention.

Perhaps this is the real reason for most of what happens in our human drama. God (our higher power, higher self, or someone out there or in here) is always trying to get our attention, to jolt us awake from the trance into which we often fall. As Henry David Thoreau wrote in *Walden*, "Only that day dawns to which we are awake."

I need to regularly wake myself up, that is, watch, listen, and do my best to understand. I must tune in to my thoughts, feelings, interactions with others, and my dreams, that is, my experience. Being mindful is a crucial first step. If I notice myself stumbling or struggling, I can connect with my source and get back on track in whatever way I find best: prayer, meditation, or maybe just a simple "Help!"

Throughout my mystical awakenings and ongoing emotional recovery, I have been learning to listen for answers to my many, ever-present questions. Sometimes, I am directed to go somewhere or do something. If I listen intently, I will hear what is even more important: Who am I? The universe and the voice within and around me regularly give hints and, at times, even proclaim loudly the truth of my own great nature. When I humbly and honestly acknowledge that, I can go nearly anywhere and do almost anything that I desire.

We do not each receive our answers in the same way. Some of us hear a voice, song, or word. Others may sense a feeling, a nudge, or an indefinable awareness. Some of us see pictures in visions and dreams. Others receive our messages in more than one way.

I am learning to trust my self, the deeper, higher part of me that is wise, loving, and concerned only with my good. When I seek for that self in the stillness, I can learn to recognize her amidst the chaos that sometimes seems to threaten my peace.

I am learning that one day, one step at a time, is the way to walk my healing journey. The next day will arrive in due time, bringing its own joys and challenges. So, I only need to take one step and then the one after that. I do not need to look far down the road. In truth, I cannot. All I can see is this moment, here and now. That is where grace abounds, the grace that lights the way to the next step if there is to be a next minute, hour, or day for me to live in this body in this place.

What about reincarnation? Did the me I know as Kathy live before? At times during my search, it seemed possible or even probable. And yet, I did not always receive immediate relief of my difficulties with the discovery of some past-life scenario. The regression experience revealed some insights that pointed me in a direction toward my healing. This recovery process may require a lot of inner work and is usually about "progress, not perfection."

A Course in Miracles says there is only now, no past or future. Now is eternity, where God exists. While that may be, in truth, our home, we find ourselves in this space/time world, where we experience our lives in a linear fashion. If there is no linear time with God, in eternity, perhaps all our lives are occurring at once in a layered fashion. I can choose to focus on an aspect (or life) of the multilayered me that seems to exist in the past but is actually outside of time. Such a concept is mind-boggling, and yet it appeals to me. It says that reincarnation may exist for us in this time/space world for purposes of self-exploration. But, in truth, now is all there really is. This theory means that those who believe in reincarnation and those who don't can both be perceived as correct.

All I can do anything about is right here in this moment. And so, to dwell unnecessarily on the past could possibly block me from accomplishing what I need to do in this incarnation. But my search for a past life did prove helpful in understanding the present. I am learning it is important for me to remain open to finding divine truth in many surprising places. The more I can empty myself of all I think I know, the more that Spirit can lead me to my ultimate healing.

No matter how much I learn, however, I cannot understand the vast, unlimited picture at this point. I have agreed to live in this limited garment of flesh. In a world of duality, clouds hide the sun's light. Yet I can still keep seeking understanding. With each cloud that is removed from the sky of our consciousness, our world becomes more enlightened.

At times, however, when the clouds of unknowing are darkest and don't seem to budge, there is something I can do. I can trust that, even though I don't see the light at that moment, the sun is still there behind the clouds. I can remember that, no matter what is happening, positive or negative, "This, too, shall pass." I can believe that I am loved always. I have been told that over and over, and I am beginning to glimpse how great our Creator's love is for us.

I am learning that we each receive what we need when we need it. I can accept that whatever I am experiencing at any moment is something that a part of me has somehow chosen. At one point, my mystical self must have needed a dolphin, a dove, a blue goddess spirit guide, and a series of visions, messages, and dreams. And so, I do not need to resist or run from or deny what is occurring in my life. I can simply be with it, whether it seems joyful, sad, ecstatic, or painful. Gratitude is an appropriate response to a pleasant experience. But gratitude is also a healing response to those events and situations, which seem lacking in love. I can trust that the sun is still shining at those dark times, also, and that there is something to learn from it.

I have had much help along my journey: my higher power, a loving husband, supportive friends and family, and, yes, for me and others, spirit guides. There are many good resources available to us, such as spiritual study groups, twelve-step groups, therapists, and churches. I have found certain practices most helpful: meditation, prayer, journaling, visualization, recording my dreams, spiritual reading, yoga, and deep breathing.

I am learning to stay in touch with my inner, deeper self. I need to regularly clear away blocks that are keeping me from living fully and confidently with joy. I simply must love myself deeply and completely. Treating my own body and personality with loving kindness is an absolute necessity on my spiritual journey. I must make every attempt, even tiny steps, to forgive myself, others, and all circumstances and events.

Dance, dance, dance! Okay! Maybe I was a little repressed. Maybe I needed to loosen up a little. Ya think? But sometimes I got awfully tired of hearing that word from my guides. When Dolfi told me to dance in the harem, I was disappointed and angry. I thought he was telling me to be sexual, and I was afraid because of my repressed wounds. What Dolfi was really saying, I now believe, was "Let go of your fears, express yourself creatively, and participate fully in the dance of life."

In my vision experience of ecstasy, I heard the words, "the cosmic dance." Life can be an ecstatic experience at times, but not if I sit on the sand and only dip my toes into the water. I have to jump in! How can I dance if I fear making a mistake, getting the steps wrong, or having other people ridicule me? I have to take a risk. I may not know the steps. I must be very still and listen. That's how I learn to hear the music of life! When I observe the birds, I know they can hear it. Their eager greeting of each new day assures me that they are in touch with the universal song.

"Come on in," they sing. "Get up! Isn't it glorious?"

Babies and children hear the music. No one has taught them yet that only particular movements are okay for certain kinds of music. Their faces light up. Their tiny arms and feet begin to sway whenever the music starts. Soon, their heads are bobbing, and their bodies are rocking. When they hear the music, they gotta dance!

Some songs that have played for me I have not yet heard, but there is no need to worry. I will hear if and when I am ready. For many years, I did not and could not hear the melody. Old habits of fear and worry had kept me gasping for breath in an effort to just stay alive, providing no extra energy for spirited movement. But Dolfi told me to dance, and my inner wisdom has reminded me over and over that I am loved and all is well. I have begun to hear the message, the music. I have been a struggling, slow learner at times. But little by little, I am learning to savor the sweetness of life, to listen for its pulsating rhythms, to wade out into the water, and, every now and then, to plunge right in.

This has been just a tiny part of my journey. I have tried to tell it as truthfully as possible. Each step has been important. And each step happens in the now. I am learning a lot about listening, trusting, and loving my higher power, my self, and others. I am learning to be grateful for each step that has gone before. I am sure that many changes lie before me. Change is, in fact, one of the only things of which I can be certain.

I know there are abundant blessings still in store for me, including more healing. And when I have completed all that is here for me to do, I will move on to the next phase of my journey, to some other place and time. And one day, I will wake up to realize that I have never left the heart and mind of my Creator, where there is no time and space, where there is only love. But while I still carry this garment of flesh, there is always more for me to learn.

I may live yet a long while on this planet, or I may leave at any moment. I could travel near and far, or my journeys may remain within my mind and heart. I do not know these things. But this I know for sure: wherever I go and no matter how old I grow, I will always remember with gratitude one amazing chapter in my story, the time when I went searching for healing and found myself dancing with the dolphin.

Bibliography

A Course in Miracles. Foundation for Inner Peace, New York, NY (Comb. Vol.) Viking, 1976

Anderson, Sherry & Patricia Hopkins. *The Feminine Face of God.*, New York, Bantam 1991

Bolen, Jean Shinoda, MD, *Goddesses in Everywoman.* San Francisco, Harper & Row 1984

Bradshaw, John. *Healing the Shame That Binds You.* Deerfield Beach, Fl: Health Comm. 1988

Bradshaw, John. *Creating Love,* New York, NY, Bantam Books, 1990

Cameron, Julia. *The Artist's Way.* New York, NY, G. P. Putnam's Sons, 1992.

Capacchione, Lucia, PhD. *The Power of Your Other Hand.*, Franklin Lakes, NJ(Rev. 2001), The Career Press

Carey, Ken. *Flatrock Journal.*, San Francisco, CA, Harper Collins, 1994.

Gray, John, PhD. *Men Are from Mars, Women Are from Venus.* New York, Harper Collins, 1992.

Kornfield, Jack. *A Path with Heart*. New York, NY, Bantam Books, 1993.

Levine, Stephen. *A Year to Live*. New York, NY Bell Tower 1997
  Who Dies. 1982 New York, NY, Random House 1982

Moody, Raymond, Jr. *Coming Back: A Psychiatrist Explores Past-Life Journeys*. New York, NY Bantam Books, 1991

Samuels, Michael, MD. *Healing with the Mind's Eye*. Hoboken, NJ, Summit Books, 1990.

Small, Jacquelyn. *Awakening in Time*. Austin TX. Eupsychian Press, 1991.

Thoreau, Henry David. *Walden*. Boston: Ticknor and Fields, 1854.

Weiss, Brian, MD. *Many Lives, Many Masters*. New York, NY, Simon & Schuster, 1988.

Zukav, Gary. *The Seat of the Soul*. New York, NY Simon & Schuster, 1989.